100
THINGS TO
KNOW ABOUT
SPACE

100
THINGS TO
KNOW ABOUT
SPACE

Written by

Alex Frith, Alice James,
& Jerome Martin

Illustrated by

Federico Mariani
& Shaw Nielsen

1 Living in the universe...

is like being on a fairground ride that never stops.

When you stand still, it doesn't feel as if you're moving. But in fact, the planet under your feet is hurtling through space at great speeds.

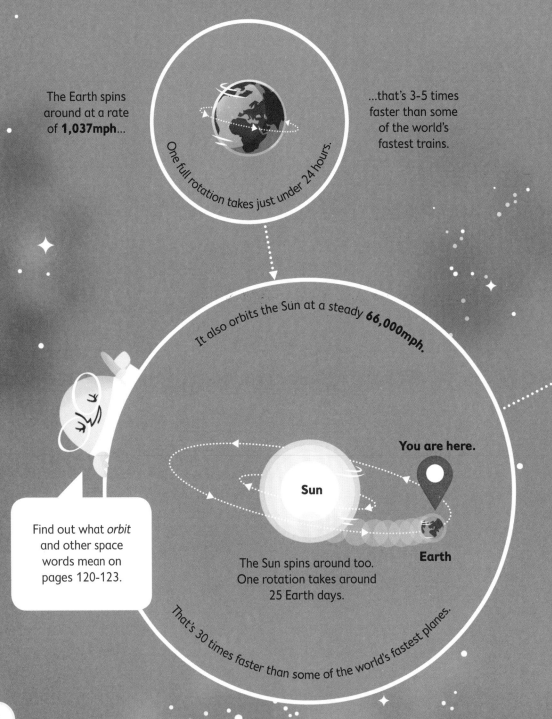

The Earth spins around at a rate of **1,037mph**...

One full rotation takes just under 24 hours.

...that's 3-5 times faster than some of the world's fastest trains.

It also orbits the Sun at a steady **66,000mph.**

Find out what *orbit* and other space words mean on pages 120-123.

You are here.

Sun

Earth

The Sun spins around too. One rotation takes around 25 Earth days.

That's 30 times faster than some of the world's fastest planes.

The Sun and the eight planets that make up the **solar system** all travel in an incredibly long *galactic orbit* around the heart of the **Milky Way galaxy**.

A single galactic orbit takes around **250 million Earth years**.

The Milky Way revolves around an object known as a **supermassive black hole**.

You are here.

The Sun

The solar system orbits at approximately **500,000mph**...

...that's 20 times faster than a rocket shooting into space.

So, we're spinning around and moving forward at the same time?

Yes. No wonder I feel dizzy.

2 The universe is *so* big...

we don't even know how big it really is.

Until 1920, astronomers believed that the Milky Way galaxy was the whole universe. Since that time, they have discovered more and more galaxies out there, stretching as far as any telescope can see.

The Milky Way is made up of at least
200 billion stars.

You are here

Local Group
– home to 54 galaxies, including the Milky Way.

Laniakea Supercluster
– a collection of over
100,000 galaxies.

Galactic superclusters
– collections of many groups of galaxies.

Voids – enormous sections of the universe with no galaxies or stars in them.

There are at least
10 million superclusters
in the universe. This means
100 billion galaxies,
bringing the total number of stars to well over
10,000,000,000,000,000,000,000.

The unknown universe

3 To be an astronaut...

you must be able to speak and read Russian.

Most astronauts fly to space on Russian rockets, with Russian writing on the controls, and half of the people on the International Space Station are Russian too. Here are a few other requirements for would-be astronauts.

You have to be able to swim.

You must be between **5ft, 3in and 6ft, 4in tall**.

You must be trained in wilderness survival.

You need a university degree in science or mathematics.

You have to be able to pilot a jet plane.

Поехали!
(*Let's go!* in Russian)

4 There are 15 sunsets every day...

on the International Space Station (ISS).

The ISS is a space station built and crewed by people from around the world. It orbits the Earth once every 92 minutes. This means that roughly every 46 minutes, astronauts on board can see the Sun rising or setting.

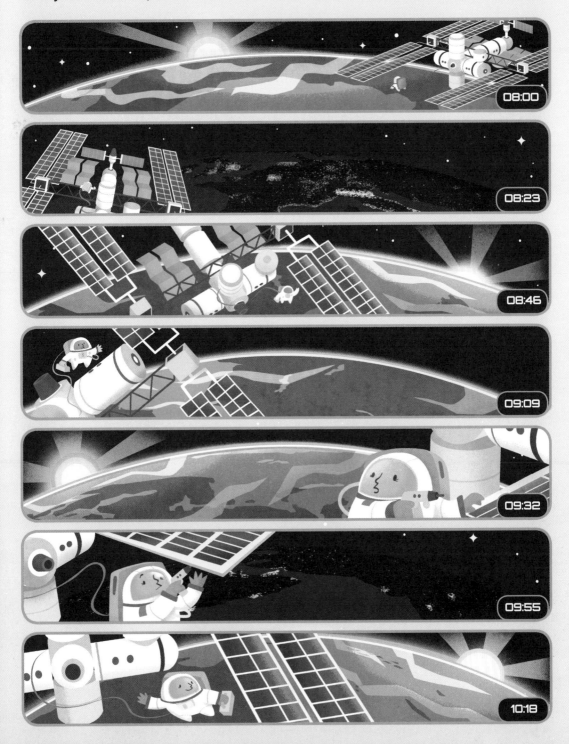

08:00

08:23

08:46

09:09

09:32

09:55

10:18

5 The Maya looked to Venus...

to plan their wars.

The ancient Maya, who lived in Central America more than 1,000 years ago, were expert astronomers. They could predict the cyclical movements of the Sun, Moon, stars and planets – often with more than **99.9%** accuracy.

They observed that the planet Venus returns to the same position on the horizon every **584 days**.

They considered **Venus** to be a **god of war**, and so they sometimes waited for key moments in Venus's cycle to launch new attacks.

Venus

The Maya discovered that the start of the 365-day Earth year coincided with the start of the 584-day Venus cycle **once every eight years**.

········· 5 Venus cycles ·········

········· 8 Earth years ·········

The Maya would have considered this a good time to raid a rival city.

6 | Someone counted the stars...

and found there are 9,096 visible in the night sky.

American astronomer **Dorrit Hoffleit** dedicated years of her life to updating a list of visible stars, known as the **Yale Bright Star Catalogue**. She discovered that, when looking from Earth in all directions, up to 9,096 stars are visible with the naked eye.

From one side of the Earth, it's only possible to see up to half the total number.

With a hand-held telescope, it's possible to see **millions** of stars.

7 There are 11 *former* planets...

in our solar system.

According to current definitions, there are just 8 planets in the Solar System. But in the past, as many as 19 different objects were described as "planets".

What's what in the solar system today

◯ Planet

◎ Dwarf planet

● Asteroid

Ten large objects in the space between Mars and Jupiter were discovered in the 1800s. At the time, they were classified as **minor planets**.

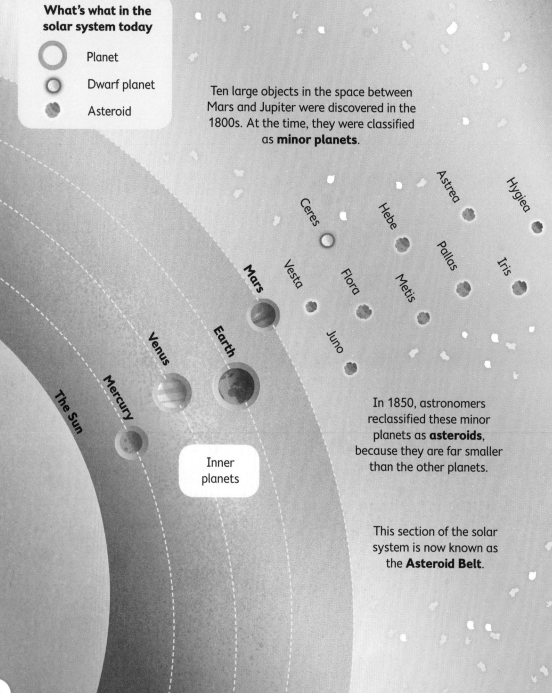

In 1850, astronomers reclassified these minor planets as **asteroids**, because they are far smaller than the other planets.

Inner planets

This section of the solar system is now known as the **Asteroid Belt**.

Astronomers discovered **Pluto** in 1930. It was bigger than any asteroid, so it was originally classified as a **planet**...

Makemake

Eris

Haumea

Uranus

Neptune

Pluto

...until 2008. By that time, astronomers discovered three new Pluto-sized objects. Instead of naming these as planets, they reclassified Pluto as a **dwarf planet**.

Saturn

Jupiter

Outer planets

When is a planet not a planet?

At the birth of the solar system, vast collections of rock and dust joined together into separate clusters of different sizes and shapes.

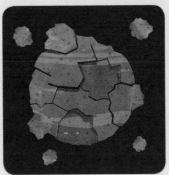

Some of these clusters were so big and heavy that their own gravity pulled them into spheres. The biggest of these are defined as planets.

As they formed, planets pulled nearby asteroids into themselves. Smaller clusters – dwarf planets – weren't powerful enough to do this.

8 The Moon is made of...

the Earth.

Scientists think the Moon was formed when an object collided with Earth, and pieces of Earth flew off into space. The biggest pieces clumped together, and formed the Moon.

Here are some of the main materials that make up the Moon and other objects in space:

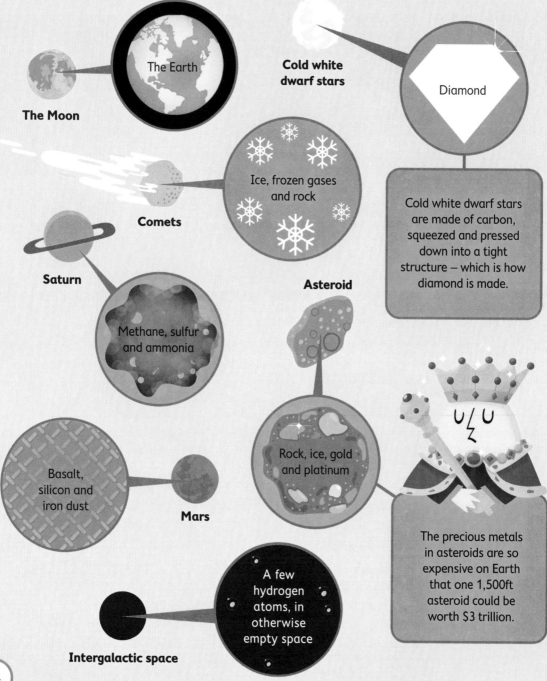

The Earth

The Moon

Cold white dwarf stars

Diamond

Ice, frozen gases and rock

Comets

Asteroid

Cold white dwarf stars are made of carbon, squeezed and pressed down into a tight structure – which is how diamond is made.

Saturn

Methane, sulfur and ammonia

Basalt, silicon and iron dust

Mars

Rock, ice, gold and platinum

A few hydrogen atoms, in otherwise empty space

The precious metals in asteroids are so expensive on Earth that one 1,500ft asteroid could be worth $3 trillion.

Intergalactic space

9 The coldest spot in space...

is right here on Earth.

These are some of the coldest known temperatures:

On the Moon:

-413°F

Temperature of the cold, dark **Hermite crater**

In space:

-457.87°F

Temperature of the rapidly expanding gases of the **Boomerang Nebula**

On Earth:

Below -459.65°F

Temperature recorded in a **laboratory** where scientists dropped **magnetized gas** down a long tower

At the theoretical limits:

-459.67°F

This is **absolute zero**: the lowest *conceivable* temperature.

Scientists have come within a few billionths of a degree of absolute zero, but it's impossible actually to reach it.

10 You can see stars in daylight...

using a radio telescope.

Stars send out all sorts of energy, including radio waves and microwaves, as well as light. Astronomers using **radio telescopes** can detect these at any time, not just at night.

Energy from a star travels in waves.

Energy moves across space in waves that can vary in size, properly called *wavelength*.

Medium-length energy waves create light we can see.

Long energy waves create microwaves.

Extra-long energy waves create radio waves.

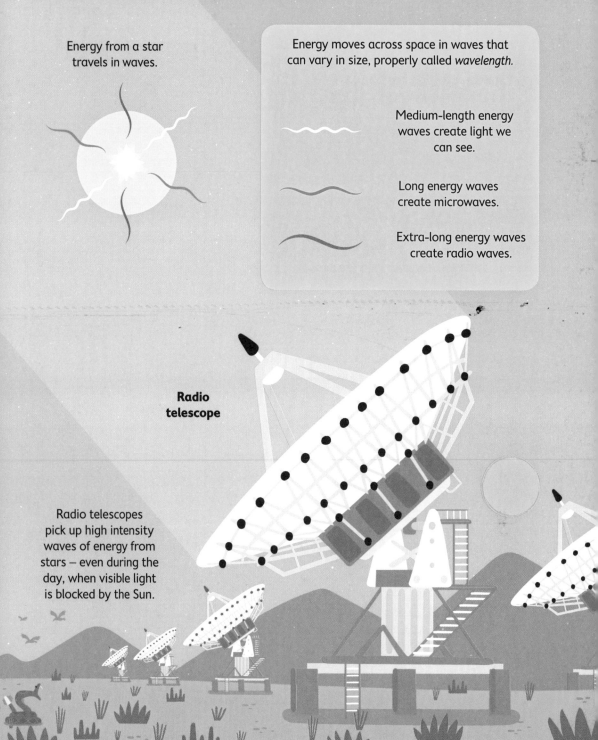

Radio telescope

Radio telescopes pick up high intensity waves of energy from stars – even during the day, when visible light is blocked by the Sun.

11 The night sky is full of light...

but we just can't see it.

The universe is infinitely large. Every direction we look in ends in a star, somewhere, which is giving off light. So the night sky should look completely light. But it doesn't.

Stars give off light, which travels in waves, called **lightwaves**.

The universe is expanding. As it does this, the distances between the stars grow. Some stars move away from us rapidly, which causes their lightwaves to stretch.

Visible light

Stretched, invisible light

The stretched wavelengths are invisible to our eyes. If we *could* see them, the night sky would be far brighter.

12 The laws of physics don't apply...
to the very first moments of time.

The universe began about **13.82 billion years ago** with an event known as the **BIG BANG** – when all of space, matter and energy swiftly and suddenly expanded out of a hot, dense speck called a **singularity**.

Over time, the universe went from being smaller than an atom...

Singularity

1 second later

...to being the size of a house to being, well, universe-sized – and it is still expanding today.

13 billion years later

Scientists have learned much about what happened during most of the first second of time. But what happened during the very first

0.000000000000000000000000000000000000000001

seconds (that's 42 zeroes after the decimal point) is still a mystery.

At that time, the universe was still so infinitesimally small, so unbelievably hot (over 100 billion degrees) and so dense...

...that there were no such things as galaxies, stars, or even atoms. Time, space, gravity and light didn't exist in forms we understand.

In that first moment, the Universe was so weird that none of today's mathematical calculations can describe it.

13 A lunar eclipse...

once helped change the course of history.

During a lunar eclipse, the Sun, Earth and Moon are temporarily aligned and the Moon turns dark as it passes through the shadow cast by the Earth.

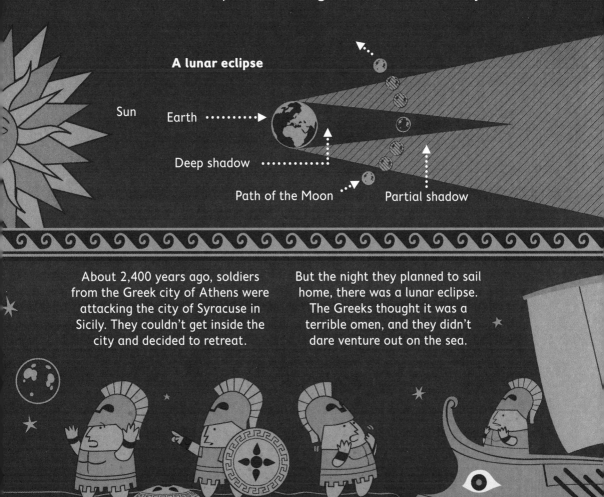

A lunar eclipse

Sun

Earth ·········▶

Deep shadow ············

Path of the Moon ····▶

Partial shadow

About 2,400 years ago, soldiers from the Greek city of Athens were attacking the city of Syracuse in Sicily. They couldn't get inside the city and decided to retreat.

But the night they planned to sail home, there was a lunar eclipse. The Greeks thought it was a terrible omen, and they didn't dare venture out on the sea.

The Syracusans took advantage of the delay and attacked the Athenian ships with their fleet. The superstitious Athenians lost the battle, their ships, and their entire army.

14 The edge of the solar system...
is a thousand times further away than Pluto.

The distance between the Earth and the Sun is so vast that scientists have come up with a new unit of measurement for it – the **astronomical unit (AU)**. This diagram shows how far some objects are from the Sun.

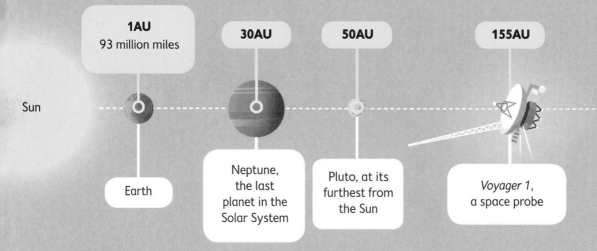

1AU
93 million miles

30AU

50AU

155AU

Sun

Earth

Neptune, the last planet in the Solar System

Pluto, at its furthest from the Sun

Voyager 1, a space probe

15 The edge of the known universe...
is 46 billion light years away from the Sun.

Distances beyond the solar system are measured in **light years (ly)**. A light year is the distance light travels in one year. As light travels incredibly fast, these distances are huge – far too big to be measured in other units.

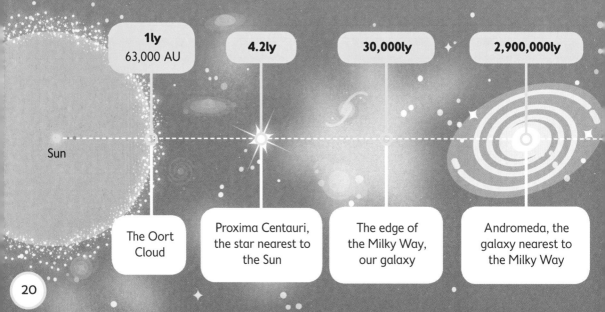

1ly
63,000 AU

4.2ly

30,000ly

2,900,000ly

Sun

The Oort Cloud

Proxima Centauri, the star nearest to the Sun

The edge of the Milky Way, our galaxy

Andromeda, the galaxy nearest to the Milky Way

63,000AU

The Oort Cloud,
a shell of icy rocks
surrounding the edge of
our solar system

46,000,000,000ly

The edge of the
known universe

16 The very first astronauts...

were fruit flies.

When scientists began developing spacecraft, they didn't know if spaceflight would be safe for humans. So they sent all sorts of other animals instead. Here are just a few of the earliest astronauts.

1947

The first animals in space: fruit flies
Launched to a height of 68 miles in a *V-2* rocket, they were recovered alive.

1949

A rhesus monkey named Albert II
Albert was the first mammal to make it to space, but he died on impact when his capsule returned to Earth.

1951

Stray dogs named Dezik and Tsygan
They were the first mammals to survive a trip to space. Dezik died on a later mission.

1959

A rabbit named Marfusha
Marfusha made it safely to space and back accompanied by two dogs.

January 1961

A chimpanzee named Ham
After one successful space mission, Ham retired to the U.S. National Zoo in Washington, D.C.

April 1961

A human named Yuri
In April 1961, following in the footsteps of dozens of animals, Yuri Gagarin became the first human to go into space.

Astronauts scratch their noses...

on a patch of Velcro® inside their helmets.

An astronaut on a spacewalk outside the International Space Station wears a special suit called an Extravehicular Mobility Unit (EMU). The EMU is equipped with all kinds of things to tackle any problem.

Gold visor to shield eyes from the glaring Sun

Lights

Heated glove fingertips, to keep hands warm

Patch of Velcro® stuck inside the helmet, for astronauts to scratch their noses on

Wrist mirror

Tether

Backwards writing on the control pack buttons, so they can be read using the wrist mirror

Jetpack attached to the back of the spacesuit, so the astronaut can zoom back to the spacecraft if the tether becomes detached

Stripes on spacesuit legs are different on every suit, so astronauts can tell each other apart.

they could have seen volcanoes erupting on the Moon.

The Moon's surface features vast, dark patches called *maria*: plains of hardened lava formed in volcanic eruptions more than a billion years ago.

However, astronomers have recently spotted a number of tiny lava plains that formed much, much later – just 50 to 100 million years ago.

This means that volcanoes were *still* erupting on the Moon during the time of the dinosaurs.

The Moon

Craters from meteoroid strikes

Volcanic eruptions

Maria

There is a cloud in outer space...

that tastes like raspberries.

Near the core of our galaxy there is a vast, bright cloud of dust and gas called *Sagittarius B2*. It is about 150 light years across, and contains countless newly formed and forming stars.

The gases and particles of dust floating in Sagittarius B2 react and combine into different types of molecules.

One molecule found throughout the cloud is **ethyl formate**. On Earth, this is what gives **raspberries** their taste.

If you could catch a mouthful of ethyl formate, it would taste a lot like a raspberry.

But you wouldn't want to taste every one of the molecules swirling through Sagittarius B2...

...because the cloud also contains a deadly chemical called **propyl cyanide**.

20 The fear of deadly Moon flu...

kept Apollo astronauts locked up for weeks.

After their spacecraft returned from the Moon in 1969, the Apollo 11 astronauts were kept in **quarantine** for three weeks. This was to stop them from spreading any unknown lunar diseases they might have caught.

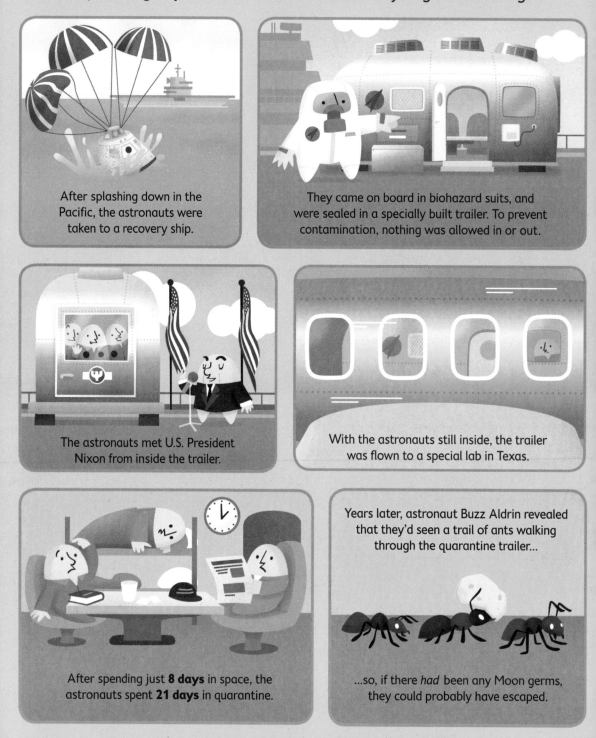

After splashing down in the Pacific, the astronauts were taken to a recovery ship.

They came on board in biohazard suits, and were sealed in a specially built trailer. To prevent contamination, nothing was allowed in or out.

The astronauts met U.S. President Nixon from inside the trailer.

With the astronauts still inside, the trailer was flown to a special lab in Texas.

After spending just **8 days** in space, the astronauts spent **21 days** in quarantine.

Years later, astronaut Buzz Aldrin revealed that they'd seen a trail of ants walking through the quarantine trailer...

...so, if there *had* been any Moon germs, they could probably have escaped.

21 A robot on Mars...

has found the building blocks of life.

A robotic, car-sized vehicle called *Curiosity* is exploring the surface of Mars. Inside it is a laboratory that tests Martian soil for the chemical ingredients that build and support life.

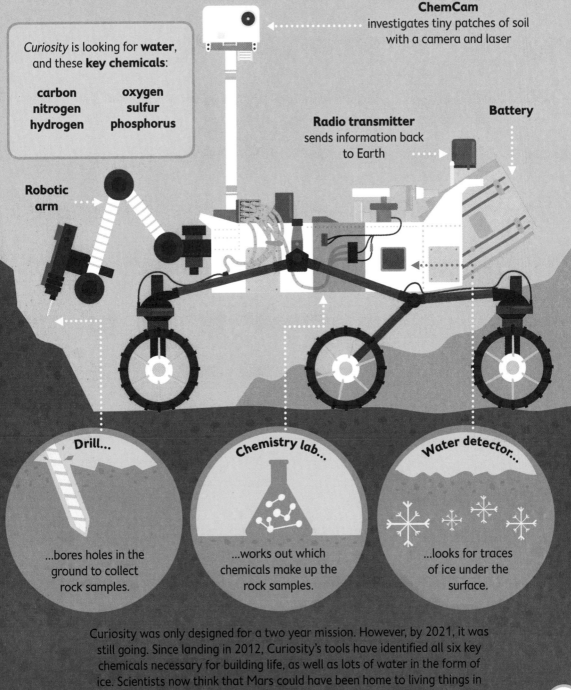

ChemCam
investigates tiny patches of soil with a camera and laser

Curiosity is looking for **water**, and these **key chemicals**:

carbon	oxygen
nitrogen	sulfur
hydrogen	phosphorus

Radio transmitter
sends information back to Earth

Battery

Robotic arm

Drill...
...bores holes in the ground to collect rock samples.

Chemistry lab...
...works out which chemicals make up the rock samples.

Water detector...
...looks for traces of ice under the surface.

Curiosity was only designed for a two year mission. However, by 2021, it was still going. Since landing in 2012, Curiosity's tools have identified all six key chemicals necessary for building life, as well as lots of water in the form of ice. Scientists now think that Mars could have been home to living things in the past – and possibly still is.

22 Astronauts on the Moon...

spent more time resting than exploring.

Although they had flown a quarter of a million miles to get to the Moon, the Apollo mission crews couldn't spend all their time exploring. To stay fit and alert, they had to schedule in long rest periods.

These graphics show how much time the astronauts of the first and last Moon missions spent eating, sleeping, working and exploring.

Key:

Working inside the Lunar Module

Exploring the Moon's surface

Eating inside the Lunar Module

Resting inside the Lunar Module

Reading order:

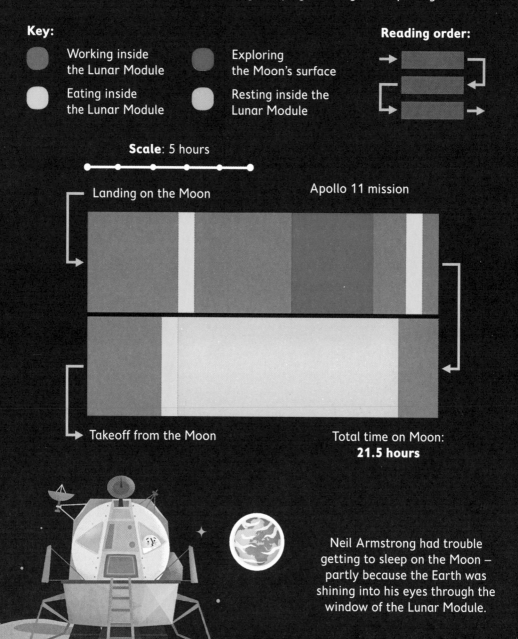

Scale: 5 hours

Landing on the Moon

Apollo 11 mission

Takeoff from the Moon

Total time on Moon: **21.5 hours**

Neil Armstrong had trouble getting to sleep on the Moon – partly because the Earth was shining into his eyes through the window of the Lunar Module.

To me, sleeping on the Moon is the greatest waste of time a human being can conceive. But we had to sleep; we were just so tired that we didn't have any choice.

– Apollo 17 commander
Eugene Cernan

Landing on the Moon

Apollo 17 mission

23 Astronomers hunt for aliens...

using equations.

Astronomer Frank Drake devised an equation to estimate roughly how many planets in our galaxy contain life that could communicate with humans. Not everyone agrees on the numbers to use, but most scientists think the **Drake Equation** is a useful starting place.

This is a simplified version of the equation. Here's how it works:

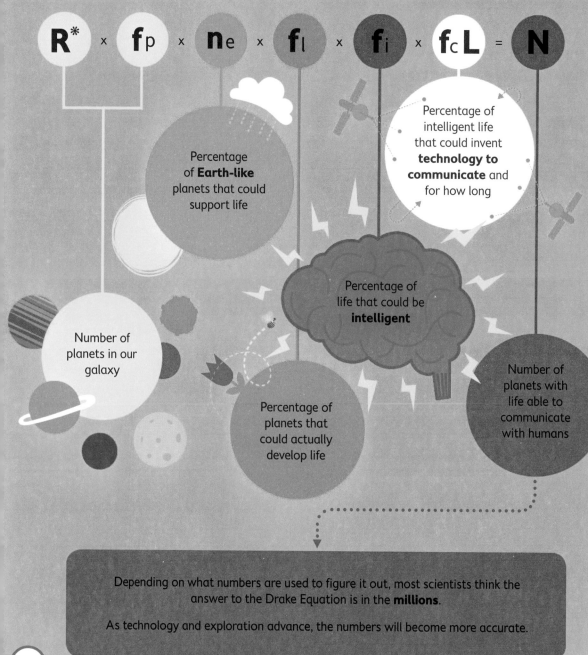

$$R^* \times f_p \times n_e \times f_l \times f_i \times f_c L = N$$

Percentage of **Earth-like** planets that could support life

Percentage of intelligent life that could invent **technology to communicate** and for how long

Percentage of life that could be **intelligent**

Number of planets in our galaxy

Number of planets with life able to communicate with humans

Percentage of planets that could actually develop life

Depending on what numbers are used to figure it out, most scientists think the answer to the Drake Equation is in the **millions**.

As technology and exploration advance, the numbers will become more accurate.

24 Dodging asteroids in space...

isn't actually very difficult or dangerous.

Movies and games set in space often show skilled pilots dodging and weaving their way past asteroids as they fly through the solar system. But, in real life, large asteroids are so far apart it's harder to *hit* one than to miss.

There's a region of space between the orbits of Mars and Jupiter that contains millions of asteroids. It's known as the **Asteroid Belt**.

Asteroids can be anything from **a few feet to 600 miles** wide.

More than 15 probes have flown through the belt without hitting anything at all.

The name makes it sound as if it's a dense ring of rocks. In fact, most asteroids in the belt are further apart from each other than Earth is from the Moon.

There's less chance of hitting an asteroid than there is of bumping into Europe or America when sailing up the Atlantic Ocean.

25 To build the first rockets...

Wernher von Braun agreed to put bombs in them.

German engineer Wernher von Braun really wanted to build spacecraft to send people to other worlds. But his first job was to design rockets that carried bombs, used during the Second World War.

1912
Wernher von Braun was born in Prussia, Germany.

1924
Young Wernher strapped fireworks to an empty wagon to make it zoom at great speeds.

1930s
Inspired by rocket science pioneer Herman Oberth, von Braun became obsessed with a few school subjects.

In von Braun's words, the rocket, "worked perfectly, but landed on the wrong planet."

1945
After the War, von Braun surrendered to the U.S. Army. They made him design new rocket missiles.

1944
During the Second World War, von Braun worked for the German government. He designed the *V-2*, a rocket-powered bomb.

1950s
The U.S. was in a race to reach space before their rivals in the Soviet Union. At long last, von Braun was asked to design a working space rocket.

1969
Von Braun's rocket, *Saturn V*, helped launch Apollo 11 — the spacecraft that took the first astronauts to the Moon.

26 All life on Earth...

may have come from outer space.

The first known living things on Earth appeared around 3.6 billion years ago. Around that time, Earth was subject to heavy bombardment from asteroids.

Earth
3.6 billion years ago

Our new home!

It's possible that some of these asteroids brought microscopic living things with them — maybe even from another planet.

Certain types of creatures — known as **extremophiles** — could survive on an asteroid with no atmosphere. The theory that life is present all over the universe, and can spread out via asteroids, is called **panspermia**.

Scientists from many different fields have championed this theory.

Hey! It was my idea first.

Lord Kelvin
Physicist
(U.K., 1870s)

Svante Arrhenius
Chemist
(Sweden, 1900s)

Chandra Wickramasinghe
Astronomer
(Sri Lanka/U.K., 1970s)

Anaxagoras
Philosopher
(Greece, 450BC)

27 The universe might look 3D...

but it is built in four dimensions.

Everything around us has **three dimensions**: length, width and height. This is true of planets and stars, too. But most scientists say the universe as a whole should be described using at least **four dimensions**.

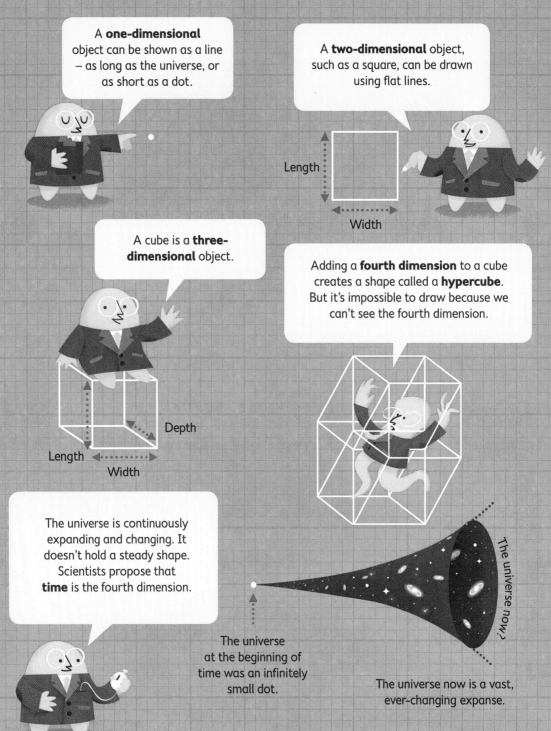

A **one-dimensional** object can be shown as a line – as long as the universe, or as short as a dot.

A **two-dimensional** object, such as a square, can be drawn using flat lines.

Length

Width

A cube is a **three-dimensional** object.

Adding a **fourth dimension** to a cube creates a shape called a **hypercube**. But it's impossible to draw because we can't see the fourth dimension.

Depth

Length

Width

The universe is continuously expanding and changing. It doesn't hold a steady shape. Scientists propose that **time** is the fourth dimension.

The universe at the beginning of time was an infinitely small dot.

The universe now?

The universe now is a vast, ever-changing expanse.

28 NASA's VAB is a building so big...

it has its own weather.

NASA's Vehicle Assembly Building (VAB) in Florida was built so that huge rockets could be assembled inside it, in a vertical position, ready to launch. It is so big that, on warm days, rain clouds can form inside.

The VAB is about **525ft** high — making it the tallest single-floor building ever built.

At
456ft
high, the VAB's doors are the largest in the world. They take 45 minutes to open.

29 Space stations and satellites...

move through space faster than the speed of sound.

There are thousands of satellites – and a space station – in orbit around the Earth. If you see them in the night sky, these objects seem to be drifting slowly around the planet. But in fact they fly very fast indeed.

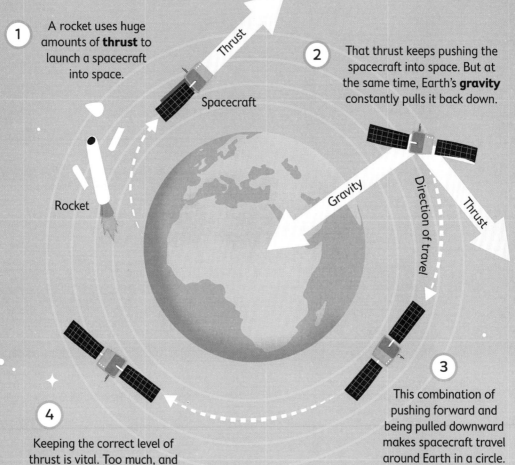

1 A rocket uses huge amounts of **thrust** to launch a spacecraft into space.

Thrust

Spacecraft

Rocket

2 That thrust keeps pushing the spacecraft into space. But at the same time, Earth's **gravity** constantly pulls it back down.

Gravity

Direction of travel

Thrust

3 This combination of pushing forward and being pulled downward makes spacecraft travel around Earth in a circle. This is known as **freefall**.

4 Keeping the correct level of thrust is vital. Too much, and the spacecraft would fly off into space. Too little, and it would fall back to Earth.

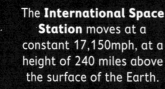

The **International Space Station** moves at a constant 17,150mph, at a height of 240 miles above the surface of the Earth.

30 Astronauts don't float...

they fall.

Being inside a spacecraft in orbit is a little like being inside a falling elevator that never reaches the ground floor.

Imagine an elevator that goes all the way up...

...into outer space.

On the journey up, the passengers feel squashed against the floor.

Earth's gravity makes the elevator start to fall. If the elevator is high enough, and moving fast enough, it will fall into orbit.

At first, this feels like falling down very fast...

...and the passengers inside start to lift off the floor. Soon, they are falling so fast they are in **freefall**.

Freefall looks and feels the same as floating.

This sensation is also known as **weightlessness**.

31 You should never grind pepper...

in space.

A space station is a virtually weightless environment, so dining there requires careful planning. Astronauts go to space with specially selected, prepared and packaged foods.

Any foods that can scatter and float around the cabin – such as tiny grains of pepper – aren't allowed.

On the International Space Station, salt and pepper come in liquid form in squeezable bottles.

To avoid crumbs, astronauts eat tortilla wraps instead of bread.

Most space food is wet and sticky. This helps the food stay put on a spoon or in a pouch.

No one is quite sure why, but living in a weightless environment dulls your sense of taste...

...so astronauts like to spice their food with hot sauce.

Food packages have Velcro® tabs, so that astronauts can stick them in place.

Magnetic knives and forks stick to metal trays, to stop them from spinning through the air.

More than a million Earths...

could fit inside the Sun.

Defined by its **volume**, the Sun is as big as 1.3 million Earths. But defined by its **weight**, the Sun is only as heavy as 333,000 Earths.

Earth is mostly made of solids and liquids, which hold close together in a tight, heavy ball.

The Sun is mostly made of gases and super-hot, **magnetized gas** known as *plasma*. These spread out to fill a gigantic ball, but compared to Earth they don't weigh very much.

33 Rocket fuel...

burns with more than twice the heat of the hottest lava.

The temperature inside a rocket engine can reach **6,000°F**.
That's hot enough to melt stone and boil iron.

Rocket engines burn fuel
to produce a stream
of very hot, rapidly
expanding gas.

The gas shoots down
through a nozzle,
pushing the rocket up
into the air.

The speed of a rocket's
exhaust can exceed
Mach 12 – that's 12
times the speed of sound.

The Earth's core is hotter...

than the surface of the Sun.

The Earth's inner core is a solid ball of super-pressurized crystalline iron. It nestles inside an outer core of cooler, molten iron.

Surface of the Sun:
9,941°F

Earth's inner core:
10,832°F

Earth's outer core:
6,872°F

Melting point of diamonds:
6,422°F

Inside a rocket engine:
6,000°F

Boiling point of gold:
5,378°F

Au

Fe

Boiling point of iron:
5,184°F

Melting point of iron:
2,800°F

Fe

Hottest lava:
2,282°F

Au

Melting point of gold:
1,947°F

35 The Space Race...

was a war without bullets.

After the Second World War, the United States and the Soviet Union became bitter rivals. Both nations competed to develop new rockets and spacecraft, to launch people into space, and eventually to explore the Moon.

BLAST OFF!

SOVIET UNION

October 1957
First artificial satellite:
Sputnik 1

SOVIET UNION

April 1961
First human in space:
Yuri Gagarin

FIRE THE BOOSTERS!
ROLL AGAIN.

LAUNCH FAILURE!
GO BACK 5 STEPS.

UNITED STATES

May 1961
First American in space:
Alan Shepard

SOVIET UNION

June 1963
First woman in space:
Valentina Tereshkova

MID-ORBIT MIX-UP!
PLAYERS SWITCH PLACES.

In space, each country could show off its technological and military power – without resorting to violence.

SOVIET UNION

February 1966
First landing on the Moon:
Luna 9 robotic probe

MID-ORBIT MIX-UP!
PLAYERS SWITCH PLACES.

SOVIET UNION

March 1965
First spacewalk:
Alexei Leonov

CCCP

UNITED STATES

December 1968
First humans to orbit the Moon: Apollo 8 astronauts

CRASH LANDING!
SKIP A TURN.

UNITED STATES

July 1969
First humans on the Moon: Apollo 11 astronauts Neil Armstrong and Buzz Aldrin

The success of the Apollo missions marked the beginning of the end of the Space Race.

MOON LANDING!

There are spies in space...

disguised as junk.

Some governments send secret satellites into space, so they can collect information about their enemies without being spotted. Everything about them is strictly classified.

The satellites are never photographed while they're being built, and they take off at night, so few people even know what they look like.

Their makers spread **disinformation** about the satellites. They might pretend they're going to be used for broadcasting television.

Once up in space they can be disguised. By turning off all signals they look unused and broken, like a piece of space junk. They can be turned back on at any moment.

They take digital photographs of P SECRET TOP SECRET TOP SECRE TOP SECRET TOP SECRET TOP SECRET T These are encrypted and sent to Earth using **transmission systems** that are almost impossible to intercept.

Inside some giant stars...

there's a tiny star hiding in the middle.

Astronomers believe that – very occasionally – a **red supergiant star** can swallow a **neutron star**. The two merge to form a type of star called a **Thorne-Żytkow object**.

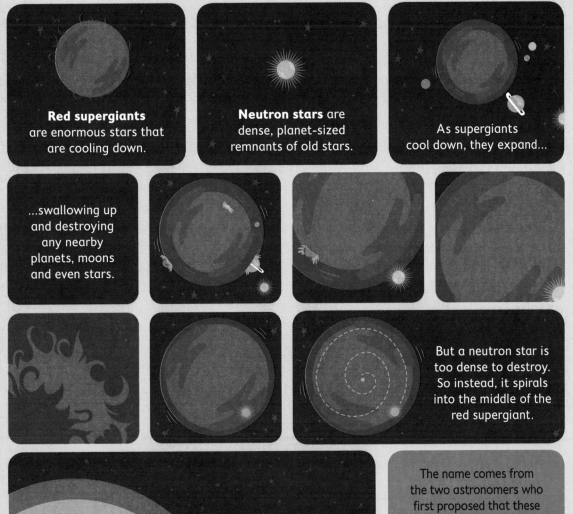

Red supergiants are enormous stars that are cooling down.

Neutron stars are dense, planet-sized remnants of old stars.

As supergiants cool down, they expand...

...swallowing up and destroying any nearby planets, moons and even stars.

But a neutron star is too dense to destroy. So instead, it spirals into the middle of the red supergiant.

Together, they become a **Thorne-Żytkow object**. This shines brighter than a red supergiant, and sends out rare chemical elements into space.

The name comes from the two astronomers who first proposed that these objects might exist.

Kip Thorne   Anna Żytkow

38 It's only a matter of time...

before a massive asteroid hits the Earth.

Hundreds of wandering asteroids zip past the Earth each year.
Hundreds more burn up harmlessly in the atmosphere.
But every 1,200 years or so, a large asteroid strikes.

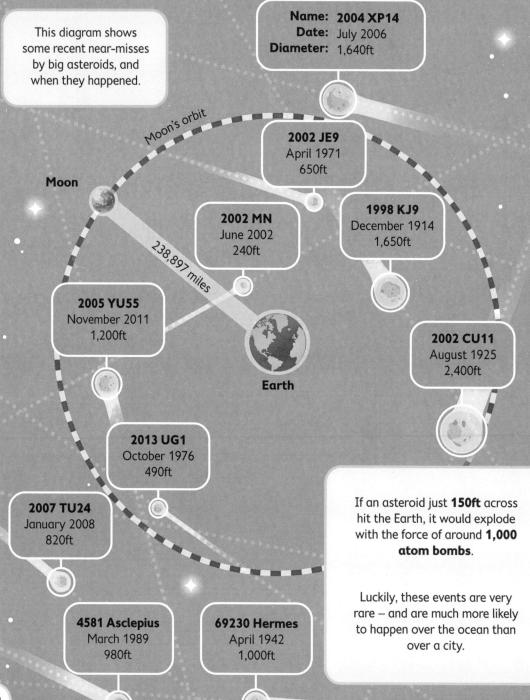

This diagram shows some recent near-misses by big asteroids, and when they happened.

Name: 2004 XP14
Date: July 2006
Diameter: 1,640ft

Moon's orbit

Moon

2002 JE9
April 1971
650ft

2002 MN
June 2002
240ft

1998 KJ9
December 1914
1,650ft

238,897 miles

2005 YU55
November 2011
1,200ft

Earth

2002 CU11
August 1925
2,400ft

2013 UG1
October 1976
490ft

2007 TU24
January 2008
820ft

If an asteroid just **150ft** across hit the Earth, it would explode with the force of around **1,000 atom bombs**.

4581 Asclepius
March 1989
980ft

69230 Hermes
April 1942
1,000ft

Luckily, these events are very rare – and are much more likely to happen over the ocean than over a city.

You could steer an asteroid...

by painting it white.

Some of the asteroids hurtling through space could potentially hit the Earth, causing massive damage. However, we may be able to steer these space rocks out of the way using nothing more than some white paint.

How it works

When rays of sunlight bounce off an object, they give it a tiny push called **radiation pressure**.

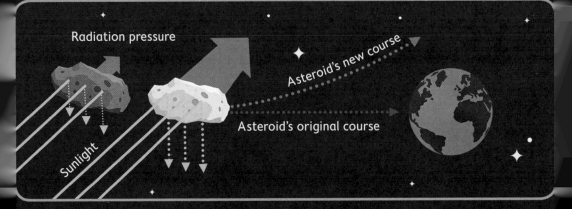

Radiation pressure

Asteroid's new course

Asteroid's original course

Sunlight

An asteroid with a white surface reflects more light than one with a dark surface, and so it experiences greater levels of radiation pressure.

Over time, this tiny change in force can add up, nudging the asteroid off its original course — and turning a potential hit into a near miss.

Moon dust is so sharp...

it can cut through spacesuits.

The Moon is covered with dust that is finer than flour, but so abrasive that it can slice through rubber and high-tech fabrics.

During the Apollo missions to the Moon, astronauts working outside became covered in dust.

The dust clogged the joints of their space suits and made it hard to move.

How dust forms on the Moon

Meteorites pepper the Moon. Wherever they strike, they melt and crush rock into microscopic, glassy particles with jagged edges.

There is no wind on the Moon, so the particles don't blow around and rub against each other. That means their edges never wear down – they stay razor sharp.

What happened next?

When the astronauts returned to their lunar lander, the dust came in with them.

It went up their noses when they breathed, and caused the first case of lunar hayfever.

They say the dust smelled — and tasted — like burned gunpowder.

The astronauts found that the dust had cut through several layers of their space boots.

Without wind to blow them away, footprints on the Moon can last for millennia.

The footprints fill up with dust at a rate of just **0.04in** every 1,000 years.

41 To fly people to Mars...

you would need to build a rocket in space.

Crewed missions to Mars will be long, dangerous and difficult. The first challenge involves the spacecraft itself. A rocket carrying enough fuel and cargo for a Mars mission would be too heavy to take off from Earth.

1. The solution would be to fly the Mars rocket into orbit, piece by piece, and assemble it there.

2. Construction crews would spend years working at something called **Low Earth Orbit** – about **250 miles** above the Earth.

The biggest structure ever assembled in orbit is the **International Space Station**. It took more than **10 years** and over **30 missions** to complete.

3. Once the Mars rocket was assembled, more rockets would carry up all the food, fuel and supplies needed for a journey of **tens of millions of miles**.

42 To survive the journey to Mars...

the crew would have to hibernate.

The journey to Mars takes **eight months**, during which astronauts would have to cope with boredom and isolation. One solution would be to put astronauts into a deep sleep.

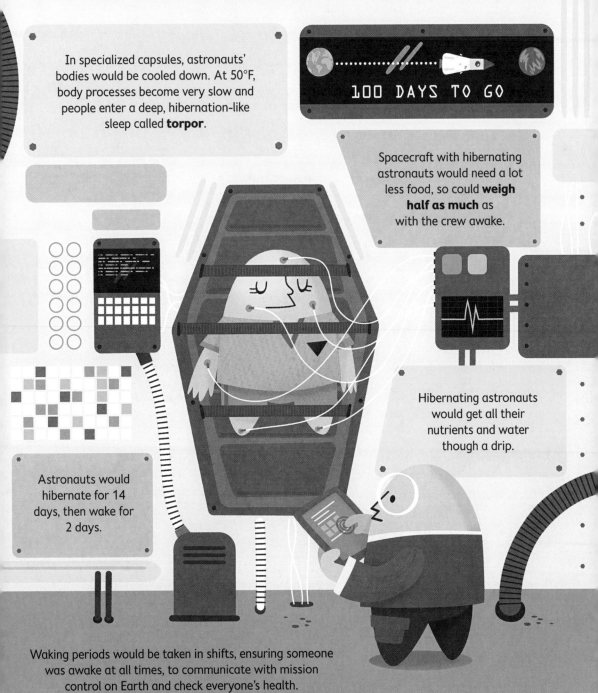

In specialized capsules, astronauts' bodies would be cooled down. At 50°F, body processes become very slow and people enter a deep, hibernation-like sleep called **torpor**.

100 DAYS TO GO

Spacecraft with hibernating astronauts would need a lot less food, so could **weigh half as much** as with the crew awake.

Hibernating astronauts would get all their nutrients and water though a drip.

Astronauts would hibernate for 14 days, then wake for 2 days.

Waking periods would be taken in shifts, ensuring someone was awake at all times, to communicate with mission control on Earth and check everyone's health.

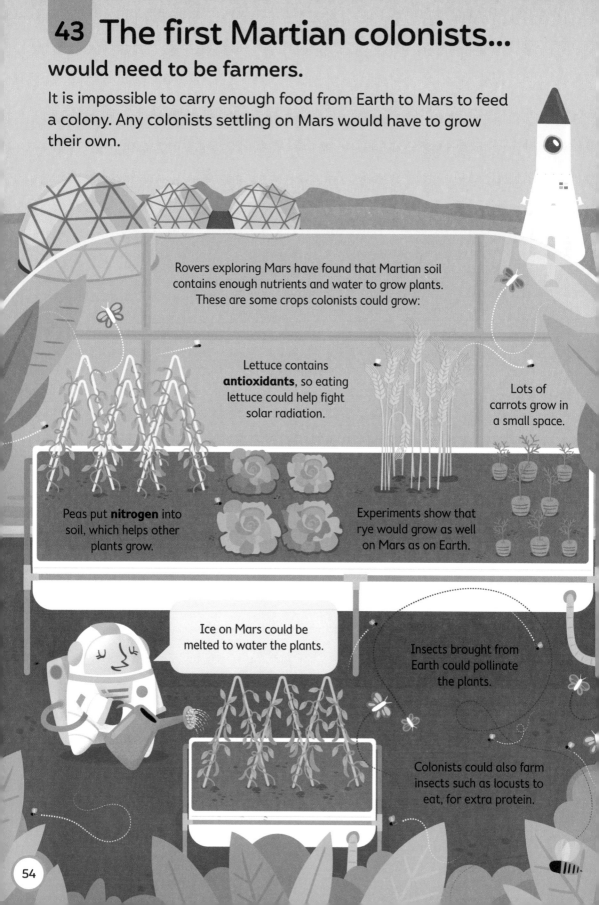

43 The first Martian colonists...

would need to be farmers.

It is impossible to carry enough food from Earth to Mars to feed a colony. Any colonists settling on Mars would have to grow their own.

Rovers exploring Mars have found that Martian soil contains enough nutrients and water to grow plants. These are some crops colonists could grow:

Lettuce contains **antioxidants**, so eating lettuce could help fight solar radiation.

Lots of carrots grow in a small space.

Peas put **nitrogen** into soil, which helps other plants grow.

Experiments show that rye would grow as well on Mars as on Earth.

Ice on Mars could be melted to water the plants.

Insects brought from Earth could pollinate the plants.

Colonists could also farm insects such as locusts to eat, for extra protein.

44 Global warming is good...

if you're planning to settle on Mars.

Dry, icy Mars cannot currently support human life. But by heating it up, humans could – over hundreds or thousands of years – make it habitable. This process is called **terraforming**, and this is how it might work:

Vast orbital mirrors could reflect sunlight onto the polar ice caps, melting the carbon dioxide ice and releasing gas to heat the atmosphere.

Asteroids rich in ammonia could be crashed into Mars, producing lots of heat. Ammonia gas would thicken the atmosphere, trapping even more heat.

Factories could be built to produce goods and materials, while pumping out methane, carbon dioxide and other gases that cause the atmosphere to warm up.

Microorganisms could be designed to survive on Mars and, like plants on Earth, could start turning carbon dioxide into breathable oxygen.

45 A ten year old girl...

discovered a dying star.

A lot of astronomical discoveries are made by people who are not professional astronomers. In 2011, ten-year-old Kathryn Aurora Gray discovered a **supernova** that no one had spotted before.

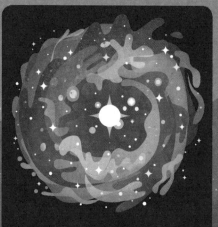

When a star runs out of energy, it explodes before it collapses and dies. This huge explosion is called a
supernova.

Kathryn made her discovery looking at online images from an observatory telescope. In one image she saw a very bright spot. This was the exploding supernova, now called *SN 2010lt*.

46 The giant planet Jupiter...

is getting smaller all the time.

Jupiter is more than twice the size of all the other planets in our solar system put together. But the planet's own structure means that it is constantly shrinking.

Jupiter has a mysterious **core** that may be made of **solid** rock.

Most of the planet is a thick layer of **hydrogen gas**...

...surrounded by a thin sheath of **helium rain**...

...and an **outer atmosphere** made up of **cool gases**.

Jupiter's core is so hot that the planet itself generates more heat than it absorbs from the Sun.

The difference in temperature between the hot core and cool outer atmosphere makes the planet shrink – but only at a rate of **1 inch** every year.

Jupiter used to be more than four times the size of all the other planets put together.

A substance no one can see...

holds galaxies together.

Stars in a galaxy are held in place by a force called gravity. Some of that gravity comes from the stars themselves, but scientists believe a lot of it comes from a mysterious, invisible substance called **dark matter**.

All objects, such as stars, have a **gravitational pull** and they exert this pull on each other.

Small stars often have a weak pull.

Big stars have a strong pull.

The middle of a galaxy is full of stars clustered together. These generate a very strong gravitational pull.

Astrophysicists know...
that galaxies spin too quickly for stars near the edge to be held in place by gravity from the middle. So there must be something else that holds them together...

Astrophysicists think... the extra gravity comes from a hidden substance called dark matter.

Dark matter is invisible, but scientists think of it as a net...

...stretching through and between galaxies.

For galaxies to work, there must be four times more dark matter than other matter.

- Dark matter
- Other matter

It's called *dark* because, unlike stars, it doesn't give off light...

...and, unlike moons and planets, it doesn't reflect light either.

48 One man found the brightest...
and darkest things in the universe.

Swiss astronomer Fritz Zwicky was the first to realize that galaxies contain completely invisible **dark matter**. He also studied the bright explosions of stars called **supernovae**. But a lot of his findings were ignored.

1898
Zwicky was born in Bulgaria, but was sent to live in Switzerland when he was just 6.

1933
Based in America, Zwicky studied galaxies. He realized that galaxies must contain invisible stuff, which we now call dark matter.

1934
Although he didn't find any, Zwicky's studies led him to believe there were super-heavy stars in space, called **neutron stars**.

To his colleagues, Zwicky was grumpy, critical and hard to work with. Some people think this is why his findings were ignored.

He linked these neutron stars to bright explosions he had observed, which he named supernovae.

Late 1940s
After the Second World War, Zwicky collected thousands of science books to give to ruined libraries around the world.

1974
By the time he died in 1974, scientists had confirmed Zwicky's theories. In 1972 he was awarded the Royal Astronomical Society's Gold Medal for lifetime achievement.

49 The first sandwich in space...

was corned beef on rye.

About two hours into the 1965 Gemini III space mission, astronaut John Young pulled a corned beef sandwich out of the pocket of his flight suit. He had smuggled it on board to share with his co-pilot Gus Grissom.

Most early space food was designed to minimize **weight**, **crumbs**, **smells** and **waste**. It was not designed to maximize taste.

A typical meal in space might include cereal cubes coated in fat, freeze-dried powders, and meat paste squeezed from a tube.

The astronauts had just a few bites of their sandwich. It was much tastier than space food...

...but it was starting to come apart — and they feared crumbs might float into sensitive cockpit electronics.

NASA administrators were not amused. Grissom and Young became the first astronauts to receive an official reprimand.

50 A space toilet costs...

$19 million.

The International Space Station (ISS) cost an estimated $150 billion up to 2010, more than anything else in history. Equipment for the ISS costs so much because it has to be specially made for use in space.

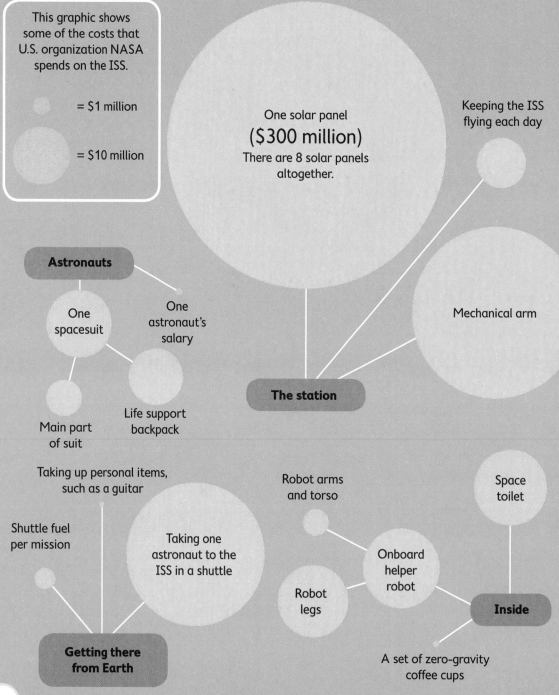

This graphic shows some of the costs that U.S. organization NASA spends on the ISS.

= $1 million

= $10 million

One solar panel
($300 million)
There are 8 solar panels altogether.

Keeping the ISS flying each day

Astronauts

One spacesuit

One astronaut's salary

Main part of suit

Life support backpack

Mechanical arm

The station

Taking up personal items, such as a guitar

Robot arms and torso

Space toilet

Shuttle fuel per mission

Taking one astronaut to the ISS in a shuttle

Robot legs

Onboard helper robot

Inside

Getting there from Earth

A set of zero-gravity coffee cups

51 Tardigrades...

are the toughest known outer space survivors.

These invertebrates, also known as moss piglets or water bears, are just **0.02 inches** long and live in damp, mossy habitats. But in a 2007 experiment, they survived more than 10 days' exposure to outer space.

They can withstand...

High pressure!

Tardigrades can withstand both the **vacuum** of space and **pressures** six times that of the deepest ocean.

Heavy radiation!

They can endure hundreds of times more **radiation** than it takes to kill a human.

Extreme temperatures!

They can survive at **304°F** and at **-458°F**, just one degree above **absolute zero**: the coldest possible temperature, at which atoms simply stop moving.

Years of drought!

They can lose **98%** of the **water** in their bodies and spend **10 years** in a state of dried-out hibernation.

Afterwards, they wake up and carry on with their microscopic lives.

To a moss piglet, it's **NO BIG DEAL.**

52 A laser battle in space...

would be dark and silent.

Movies and comics set in space often play fast and loose with scientific accuracy, to make the action more exciting to look at, and easier to follow. But scenes like the one shown here could never happen in real life.

Sound needs a substance to move through — but space is empty, so it's silent.

You wouldn't see spacecraft engulfed in flames, because there is no oxygen in space to burn.

SWOOOOSHH

PEW PEW

PEW PEW

PEW PEW PEW PEW

BOOOOM

Lasers move at the speed of light. It's impossible to dodge something that fast.

PEW PEW

PEW PEW

From the side, laser beams are invisible — unless their light bounces off dust or gas clouds.

WHIRRRR

There's no air in space, so spacecraft don't need aerodynamic shapes to change direction quickly.

THRRRRMM

NYAAOOWWWW

64

Patterns of stars...

are just tricks of the mind.

Astronomers group the brightest stars in the night sky into patterns called **constellations**. But although they look close together from Earth, the stars that make them up can be far, far apart.

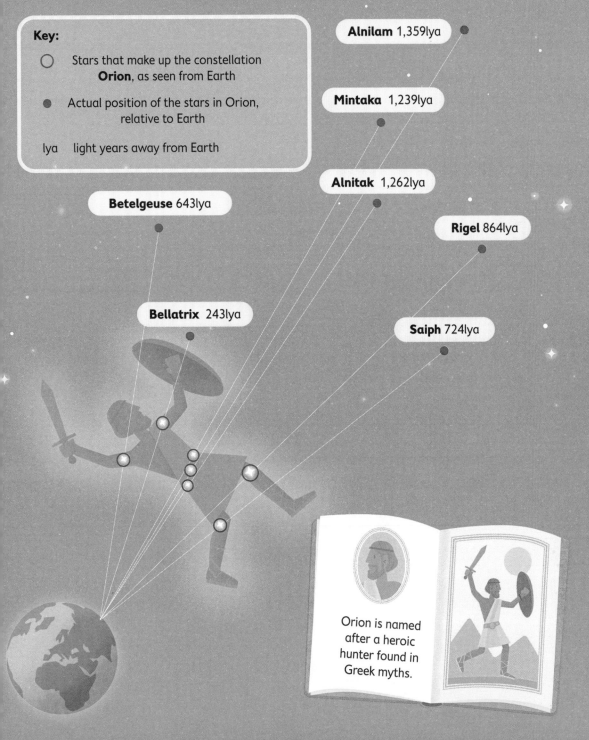

Key:

○　Stars that make up the constellation **Orion**, as seen from Earth

●　Actual position of the stars in Orion, relative to Earth

lya　light years away from Earth

Alnilam 1,359lya

Mintaka 1,239lya

Alnitak 1,262lya

Betelgeuse 643lya

Rigel 864lya

Bellatrix 243lya

Saiph 724lya

Orion is named after a heroic hunter found in Greek myths.

54 Neil Armstrong's boots...

are still up on the Moon.

Before flying back to Earth, the Apollo 11 astronauts dumped everything they no longer needed on the lunar surface. In total, humans have left more than **400,000lbs** of litter on the Moon.

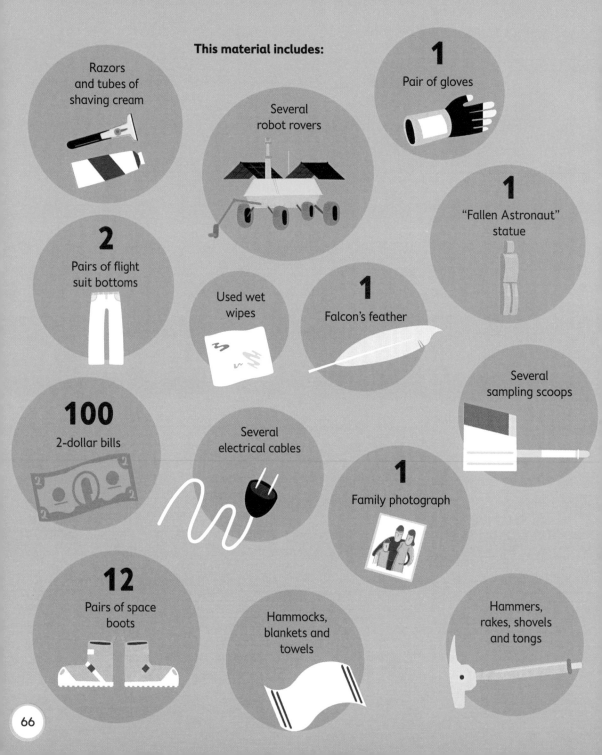

This material includes:

Razors and tubes of shaving cream

Several robot rovers

1
Pair of gloves

1
"Fallen Astronaut" statue

2
Pairs of flight suit bottoms

Used wet wipes

1
Falcon's feather

Several sampling scoops

100
2-dollar bills

Several electrical cables

1
Family photograph

12
Pairs of space boots

Hammocks, blankets and towels

Hammers, rakes, shovels and tongs

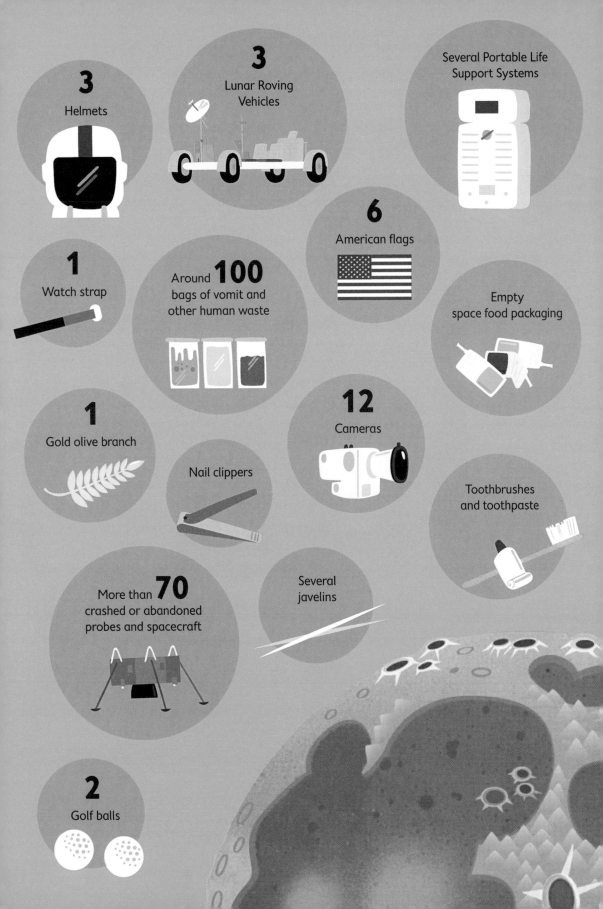

3
Helmets

3
Lunar Roving Vehicles

Several Portable Life Support Systems

6
American flags

1
Watch strap

Around **100** bags of vomit and other human waste

Empty space food packaging

1
Gold olive branch

Nail clippers

12
Cameras

Toothbrushes and toothpaste

More than **70** crashed or abandoned probes and spacecraft

Several javelins

2
Golf balls

55 Neptune was discovered...

by mathematicians, not stargazers.

Neptune was first confirmed as a planet in 1846 by an astronomer using a telescope. But he only knew where to look thanks to calculations provided by a mathematician.

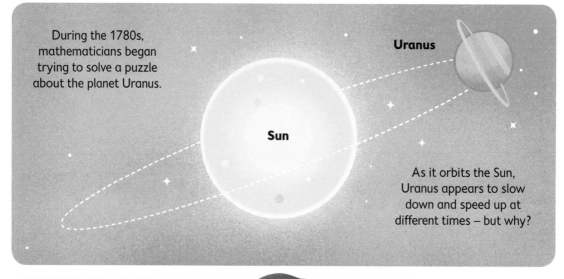

During the 1780s, mathematicians began trying to solve a puzzle about the planet Uranus.

Uranus

Sun

As it orbits the Sun, Uranus appears to slow down and speed up at different times – but why?

In 1821, astronomer **Alexis Bouvard** suggested one possible reason:

A large, as yet unknown, planet is pulling on Uranus as they pass close to each other.

In the 1840s, two rival mathematicians – **Urbain Le Verrier** and **John Couch Adams** – calculated the location such a planet would have to occupy in space.

Stop copying me!

Le Verrier

Adams

In 1846, astronomer **Johann Galle** followed Le Verrier's prediction, and found Neptune just a few degrees away.

56 Inches, ounces and pounds...

can crash a spacecraft.

In 1999, NASA's unmanned *Mars Climate Orbiter* completed its 9-month journey to Mars.

Mars

ERROR

But instead of orbiting the planet as planned, it flew into Mars's upper atmosphere and disintegrated.

How did this happen?

Most people working on the *Orbiter* made calculations using the **metric system** – which measures distance in meters and mass in kilograms.

But one team instead mistakenly used **US customary units** – a system that measures distance in feet and inches and mass in pounds.

This mix-up meant the estimated distance between Mars and the $125 million *Orbiter* was disastrously wrong.

We are on a collision course...

with the Andromeda Galaxy.

Our galaxy, the Milky Way, is around 2.5 million light years away from the Andromeda Galaxy. But they are approaching one another at a rate of around 68 miles per second.

1

The Milky Way and Andromeda are predicted to cross paths in roughly **four billion years**.

The Milky Way

Andromeda

2

Because the stars in each galaxy are spread so far apart, there probably won't be any dramatic crashes or explosions.

3

The galaxies will sweep right through one another, like a swirling mist passing through a sprinkle of rain.

4

But their fates are intertwined. Their combined gravity will keep pulling them closer and closer until, eventually, they merge to form a single **supergalaxy**.

Milkdromeda

58 Astronauts drink...

the same water again and again and again.

Sending water supplies into orbit is wildly expensive. To conserve as much as possible, the astronauts on the International Space Station use a recycling system that can reclaim **93%** of the water on board.

1 The recycling system dispenses clean, fresh water for the astronauts to drink.

6 Then it filters and distills the water so that it's purer than the water we drink on Earth.

2 The astronauts breathe out water as **moist air**...

The space station's recycling system can provide water for **six astronauts** for more than **three years** without resupply.

3 ...and expel it as **sweat**...

5 The recycling system collects water and sucks moisture from the air.

4 ...and pass it as **urine**.

59 Space holds many dangers...
but no one knows exactly which danger kills first.

Without protective clothing, a person in space would be exposed to at least three lethal situations. Each one of these could kill in as little as 60 seconds.

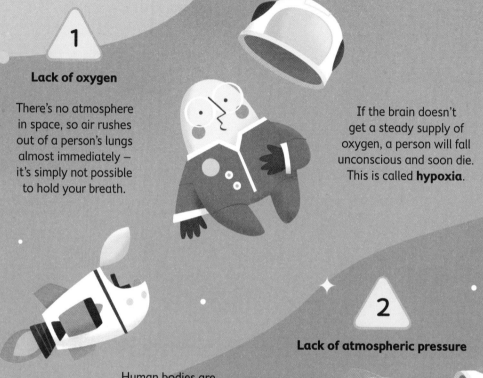

1

Lack of oxygen

There's no atmosphere in space, so air rushes out of a person's lungs almost immediately — it's simply not possible to hold your breath.

If the brain doesn't get a steady supply of oxygen, a person will fall unconscious and soon die. This is called **hypoxia**.

2

Lack of atmospheric pressure

Human bodies are designed to cope with the **air pressure** in Earth's atmosphere.

When there's not enough pressure, bubbles of gas form rapidly inside blood and bones, and the whole body swells up a little.

In just 90 seconds, there are enough bubbles to block blood flow through the body. This is called **ebullism**.

Safety on Earth

Earth is covered by a thick **atmosphere** of oxygen and other gases. The whole planet is surrounded by a **magnetic field**.

Together, these help keep lifeforms alive.

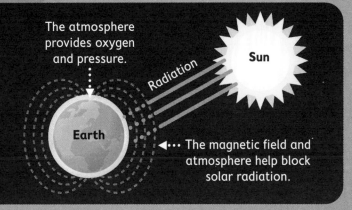

The atmosphere provides oxygen and pressure.

Radiation

Sun

Earth

⬅⋯ The magnetic field and atmosphere help block solar radiation.

3

Exposure to radiation

The Sun gives off **cosmic rays** that damage body cells, as well as **ultraviolet radiation** that rapidly burns the skin.

Spacesuits mimic the conditions people experience on Earth.

Opening the suit would be fatal – although no one knows exactly *which* of the three fatal dangers would be the direct cause of death.

60 A student's discovery...

was stolen by her professor.

Until the 1920s, most astronomers believed that the Sun was made mostly of the same stuff as planet Earth. PhD student Cecilia Payne proved them wrong.

1900
Cecilia Payne was born in Wendover, U.K.

1919
She studied science at Cambridge University – but the university didn't allow women to graduate.

1923
Payne moved to the U.S. to study at the Harvard Observatory, where she began a PhD in astronomy.

The Sun is made of...

Hydrogen
70%

Helium
28%

Other elements
2%

1925

As part of her research, Payne studied light from the Sun. She discovered that it wasn't made of rock or metal, like the Earth, but was mostly **hydrogen**. *Senior astronomer Henry Russell advised her not to present this controversial finding in her PhD.*

1929
Russell completed his own analysis of the Sun. He proved that Payne was right – but took most of the credit himself.

1930s-1960s
Under her married name, Payne-Gaposchkin, she devoted her life to astronomy, measuring light from over two million stars.

1979
By the time she died, Cecilia Payne-Gaposchkin had paved the way for women to study astronomy, and other sciences, across the world.

61 Noise from the Big Bang...

was first mistaken for pigeon droppings.

In 1963, two US astronomers noticed that their radio telescope was picking up persistent, low-level interference or static. At first, they blamed it on the droppings left inside the telescope by nesting pigeons.

But when they got rid of the birds and scrubbed the telescope clean, the static was still there.

It wasn't interference at all: it was a signal from deep space. It could be found in every direction they aimed the telescope.

In fact, the astronomers were picking up the distant echoes of the **Big Bang** – the event that created **time** and **space**.

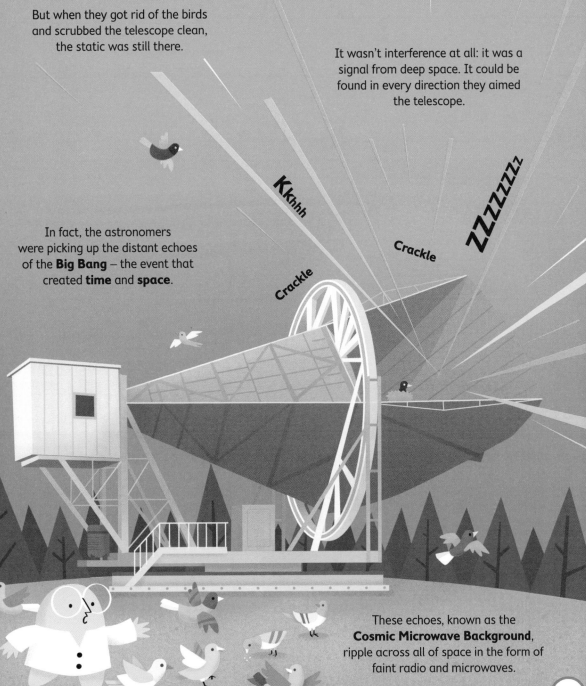

Kkhhh

Crackle

Crackle

Zzzzzzz

These echoes, known as the **Cosmic Microwave Background**, ripple across all of space in the form of faint radio and microwaves.

62 Astronomers listen to the Sun...

to find out what's inside.

The Sun is made up of gases and plasma that constantly swirl and ripple. To understand what's going on inside, astronomers use computers to translate those ripples and swirls into sound waves.

From a distance, the Sun appears to be a silent yellow ball.

But deep inside, swirling energies force sound waves through the Sun...

...making the whole thing ring like a bell.

Sound can't travel through space, but as the Sun "rings", it makes light move in subtle pulses.

Astronomers use computers to convert these pulses of light into waves of sound.

These sound waves allow astronomers to form a picture of what's inside the Sun. This technique is called **helioseismology**.

The technique reveals hidden layers of the Sun.

Corona

Core

Photosphere

Chromosphere

63 Spaghettification...

is what happens if you get too close to a black hole.

Black holes are the remnants of giant stars that have exploded. Their gravitational pull is so strong it can pull objects into long, thin strands.

The edge of a black hole is an imaginary line called an **event horizon**. Spacecraft can orbit around an event horizon safely...

...but only if they're flying nearly as fast as the speed of light (a feat well beyond current technology).

Event horizon

If a spacecraft fell inside the event horizon, the force of gravity would be so powerful that it couldn't escape. The front end would get pulled in faster than the back end, so the craft would get drawn out – like a strand of spaghetti.

64 The man in the Moon...

is also a rabbit and a frog.

Throughout history, and all over the world, people have identified all kinds of different shapes on the surface of the Moon. These are examples of a type of illusion known as **lunar pareidolia.**

The dark patches on the Moon are actually caused by volcanic rock and shadows from deep meteor craters. People from different cultures visualize these patterns in a variety of different ways.

علي

In China and Japan, people often describe seeing a rabbit mashing rice in a pot.

Folk tales about the Moon from parts of Africa, and North America, describe a leaping frog.

In western European countries, many old stories tell of a man on the Moon, carrying a bundle of sticks.

In Arabic-speaking countries, many people see letters. They spell out the name *Ali*, one of the founding figures of Islam.

65 A message to aliens...

has been beamed into space.

Astronomers have sent messages into space in an attempt to communicate with aliens. To read them, aliens will need to understand a human code.

This message, called *Arecibo*, was sent in 1974 from a radio telescope. It was transmitted as a series of 0s and 1s, which can also be represented visually.

The Arecibo message was designed to be broken down and represented in pictures. It contained pieces of information about human life, including:

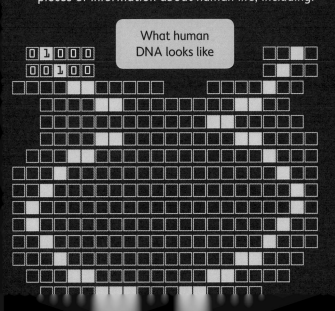

What human DNA looks like

A human's body shape

Saturn collects comets...

and turns them into rings.

Saturn's rings are made from trillions of orbiting chunks of ice. They are the remains of icy **comets**, **moons** and **asteroids** pulled in by Saturn's gravity and broken apart in violent collisions with each other.

Some of the chunks of ice are as small as grains of sand, and some are as big as houses. Most would fit in the palm of your hand.

Although Saturn's rings have a diameter of around **155,000 miles**, in most places they are just **33 feet** thick.

Earth

Saturn's rings
(seen from the side)

Saturn
(seen from the side)

7,900 miles

155,000 miles

Close-up of Saturn's rings

Saturn's rings
33 feet thick

London bus
37 feet long

Bowhead whale
65 feet long

Pieces of ice floating in the rings can clump together, forming tiny **moonlets**. Over time, they may grow into icy moons, like the four below, and migrate into wider orbits.

So far, scientists have identified around **53 moons** orbiting Saturn – but that number may increase.

Saturn's rings
(seen from above)

Tethys

Enceladus

Saturn
(seen from above)

Mimas

Pan

Some tiny moons, such as **Pan**, orbit within the rings, keeping their lanes open by sweeping chunks of ice out of their paths.

67 The Sun isn't yellow...

it's actually bright white.

Light from the Sun travels in waves. These are distorted by the Earth's atmosphere in a process known as **Rayleigh scattering**. This is what makes the Sun appear warm and yellow in the sky.

Earth's atmosphere

The Sun

Earth

Never look at the Sun directly as this can damage your eyes.

68 Opportunity bounced...

to land on Mars.

Robotic vehicles called rovers have been sent to explore Mars. Some of them, including one called *Opportunity*, landed by bouncing off the surface.

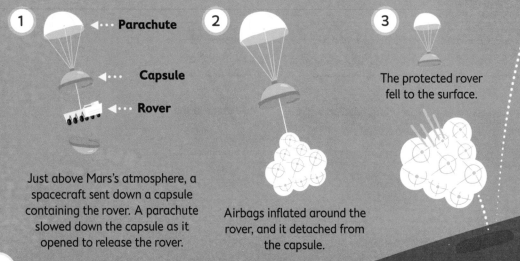

1. Parachute

Capsule

Rover

Just above Mars's atmosphere, a spacecraft sent down a capsule containing the rover. A parachute slowed down the capsule as it opened to release the rover.

2. Airbags inflated around the rover, and it detached from the capsule.

3. The protected rover fell to the surface.

Although the Sun looks white in space, each ray is actually made up of a rainbow, or **spectrum**, of different sorts of light.

Molecules

When the Sun's rays hit dust and gas molecules in Earth's atmosphere, the spectrum is scattered.

Dust

The rays that reach us directly are mostly yellow.

The Sun

Blue and violet rays scatter widely, making the sky appear blue.

The rover *Opportunity* was designed to investigate Mars for **90** days, but continued exploring for **15** years.

4

The first time it hit the surface, it bounced

39ft

back up.

5

Then it bounced more than

20

times...

...before rolling to a stop.

When it stopped, the airbags deflated and fell away, so the rover could start to explore.

6

69 Where outer space begins...

isn't entirely clear.

As spacecraft take off from Earth, the air around them gets thinner, fading into outer space. But there's no clear border between *atmosphere* and *space* – so astronauts might not know when they get there.

Over the years, military and scientific groups have proposed several definitions of where space begins.

50 miles above sea level

Some say space begins here – where the air becomes so thin that it won't support the wings of most planes.

62 miles

This is known as the **Kármán Line**. It is named after a scientist who calculated that even rocket-powered aircraft couldn't fly past this point. Only spacecraft could travel further.

Wait – are we in space yet?

80-90 miles

This zone marks the closest that an orbiting satellite can come to Earth. Any closer, and the thicker atmosphere would act as a brake, slowing the satellite and eventually bringing it back down to Earth.

430 miles

This is where the very outer part of Earth's atmosphere – the **exosphere** – begins. This zone is both part of Earth and part of space, and extends to a distance of 6,200 miles. Here, atoms that make up the air can travel thousands of miles without bumping into one another.

70 Snow on Mars...

is square.

Most of the atmosphere around Mars is made of **carbon dioxide gas**. In cold Martian winters, this freezes and turns into clouds of tiny, almost cube-shaped crystals called **dry ice**. Dry ice can fall like snow.

On Earth, crystals of water form intricate snowflakes.

Crystals of carbon dioxide form miniscule cube-like shapes.

There are permanent ice caps at the poles on Mars, just as on Earth. They are mostly made of water ice, with a covering of dry ice in winter.

71 Cosmonauts used to be armed...

to fight off wolves and bears.

Even if they survived the dangers of early space missions (such as explosive rocket launches and pioneering spacewalks), Russian cosmonauts returning to Earth could still come face to face with a pack of wolves or a hungry bear.

When space capsules re-enter the atmosphere, they deploy parachutes to make a soft landing.

But early capsules were so hard to steer that they would sometimes drift hundreds of miles off course.

Some cosmonauts overshot their landing zones and parachuted into the dense, snowy forests of northern Russia.

There, surrounded by prowling animals, they had to camp out until search parties could reach them on skis or by helicopter.

Many missions were equipped with a special **survival weapon**: a gun with three barrels that could shoot rescue flares, shotgun shells and bullets.

72 Technology made for the Moon...

can now be found in people's homes.

In the 1960s, Apollo astronauts used a revolutionary cordless electric drill on the Moon's surface. Back on Earth, that technology led to the invention of the first cordless vacuum cleaner.

Here are some more examples of everyday technology designed for use in space:

Scratch-resistant coatings

Special coatings first tried out on space helmet visors are now used to protect glasses.

Artificial limbs

Technology developed for robot rovers is now used to make better artificial limbs.

Heat-resistant materials

Materials invented for shielding spacecraft also keep firefighters safe on Earth.

Freeze-dried foods

Lightweight, nutritious freeze-dried foods are eaten both by astronauts and hikers.

A wormhole...

could shoot you through space and time.

In theory, a **wormhole** is a tunnel linking two places in the universe. No one knows if wormholes really exist, but scientists agree that they *could*. If we found one, we could use it as a passage through space and time.

Astrophysicists believe that strong fields of gravity can warp space, and tear holes in it. If two of these holes connected, they could form a wormhole through the universe.

It's called a wormhole because it's like a hole eaten through an apple by a worm.

But wormholes present a few problems. They would be:

...microscopically small,

...they might collapse,

...and there's no way of knowing when or where the wormhole might lead to.

So if you went through a wormhole you might pop up somewhere millions of years in the future...

...or in a distant galaxy, deep in the past.

74 If the Sun burned out today...

it would still shine for another million years.

The Sun generates heat and light when its atoms collide and fuse together. But even if they stopped suddenly, there would still be enough energy inside the Sun for it to keep on radiating for a long time.

The inside of the Sun is a little like a giant labyrinth. Light and heat are generated in the Sun's **core**, and have to find their way to the surface.

Light zooms around inside the body of the Sun, following paths that can take **millions of years** to reach the surface.

Heat moves in steady waves from the core to the surface. This process can take years.

Once at the Sun's surface, **heat and light** can travel in a direct line to Earth, taking just over **8 minutes** to cross space.

Don't worry!
The Sun isn't going to stop shining for at least **5 billion years**.

75 Metals in space...

can fuse together spontaneously.

When astronauts do repairs outside space stations, they have to be very careful not to touch two separate metal objects together. This is because they can fuse together instantly. Here's how:

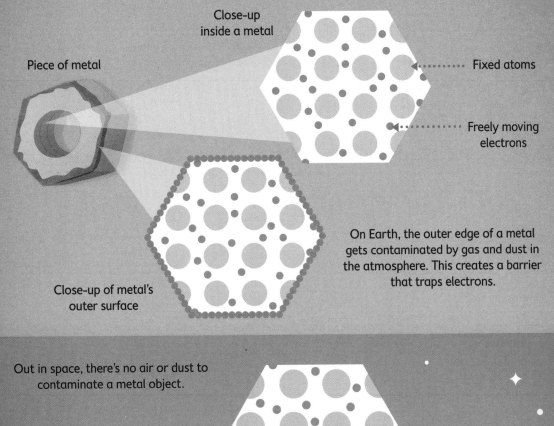

Close-up inside a metal

Piece of metal

Fixed atoms

Freely moving electrons

Close-up of metal's outer surface

On Earth, the outer edge of a metal gets contaminated by gas and dust in the atmosphere. This creates a barrier that traps electrons.

Out in space, there's no air or dust to contaminate a metal object.

When two pieces of clean metal touch, the electrons immediately move freely between them...

...creating one single fused piece.

Grr! Not again. Next time I'll use a plastic one.

Moon golf...

was the first extraterrestrial sport.

In 1971, the Apollo 14 astronaut Alan Shepard brought
two golf balls and a golf club to the Moon.

Gravity on the Moon isn't as strong as on the Earth...

Shepard's spacesuit was
stiff and bulky, so he used
a one-handed swing.

The club was made using the
head of a six-iron and the handle
from a sampling scoop.

...so the ball flew far over the lunar surface.

Today, the golf club is in a
golfing museum on Earth.
The balls are still on the Moon.

77 Humans *could* colonize Europa...

but you'd better think twice before booking a visit.

Europa is one of Jupiter's moons. Scientists believe there is a salty sea beneath its outer crust of ice, and that humans could live there some day.

SEE THE SALTWATER GEYSERS

20 TIMES TALLER THAN EVEREST

EUROPA: UNBEATABLE JUPITER VIEWS

UNDER ICE 100 MILES THICK

VISIT THE
UNDERWATER CAPITAL

TERMS AND CONDITIONS

- AVERAGE ROUND TRIP: 12 YEARS

- EUROPA SURFACE TEMPERATURE: -275°F

- EUROPA SURFACE RADIATION LEVELS: 108% FATAL HUMAN DOSE EVERY DAY

- LOW EUROPA GRAVITY MAY CAUSE: LOSS OF MUSCLE, BONE DENSITY AND VISION

- EUROPA'S SEA MAY CONTAIN: UNKNOWN ALIEN CREATURES

- ICE-PLATE TECTONICS MAY CAUSE: ICE-QUAKES

- SURVIVAL NOT GUARANTEED

78 A day on Mercury...

lasts nearly as long as a year.

Planet Mercury spins around very slowly, but it orbits the Sun very quickly. Compared to Earth, a day lasts for ages, but a year flies by.

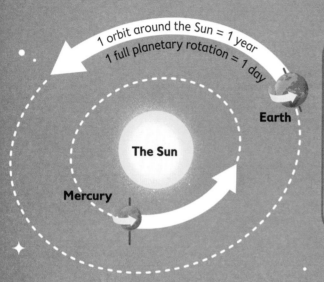

1 orbit around the Sun = 1 year
1 full planetary rotation = 1 day

Earth

The Sun

Mercury

	Length of Day	Length of Year
Earth	24 hours (1 Earth day)	8,760 hours (365 Earth days)
Mercury	1,407 hours (58 Earth days)	2,112 hours (88 Earth days)

A whole year goes by on Mercury in the same time as one and a half Mercury days.

79 You wouldn't need a parachute...

to go cliff-jumping on Miranda.

The surface of Miranda, a small moon of Uranus, is riddled with deep canyons.

I've been falling down for 10 minutes!

The pull of gravity here is **less than a hundredth** of Earth's gravity. So if you jumped off a cliff into one of its canyons, you'd fall very slowly and land gently.

80 There is a graveyard in space...

for old spacecraft.

Satellites orbiting the Earth get old and broken, just as cars do. When they become too old or broken to use, they enter an orbit full of disused spacecraft called the **Graveyard Orbit**.

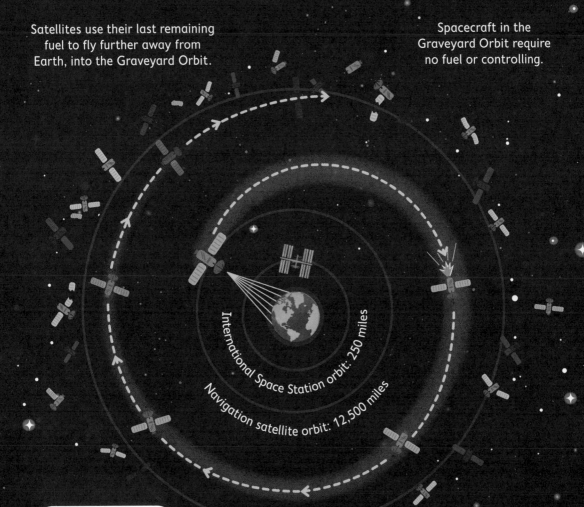

Satellites use their last remaining fuel to fly further away from Earth, into the Graveyard Orbit.

Spacecraft in the Graveyard Orbit require no fuel or controlling.

International Space Station orbit: 250 miles

Navigation satellite orbit: 12,500 miles

Graveyard orbit: 22,400 miles

There are also 500,000 small pieces of space junk floating around Earth.

If a piece of space junk collided with a working spacecraft it could cause enormous damage. NASA tracks anything larger than a tennis ball, so spacecraft can dodge these dangerous objects.

81 Everything orbited the Earth...

until Galileo discovered the moons of Jupiter.

For hundreds of years, people believed that the Earth was the middle of the universe, and that everything else (including the Sun) revolved around it. This theory is known as **geocentrism**.

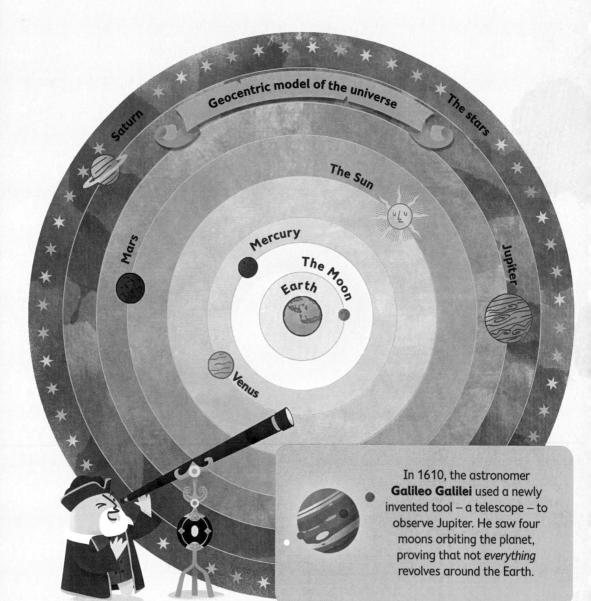

Geocentric model of the universe

The stars

Saturn

The Sun

Mars

Mercury

The Moon

Earth

Jupiter

Venus

In 1610, the astronomer **Galileo Galilei** used a newly invented tool – a telescope – to observe Jupiter. He saw four moons orbiting the planet, proving that not *everything* revolves around the Earth.

Galileo's discovery helped astronomers show that the Earth and the other planets in the solar system orbit the Sun. This theory is called **heliocentrism**.

82 The Sun is tiny...

compared to other stars.

Although the Sun is huge compared to Earth, there are much larger stars out there. These can be so huge that scientists have invented a special unit of measurement for them – the **solar radius** (R☉).

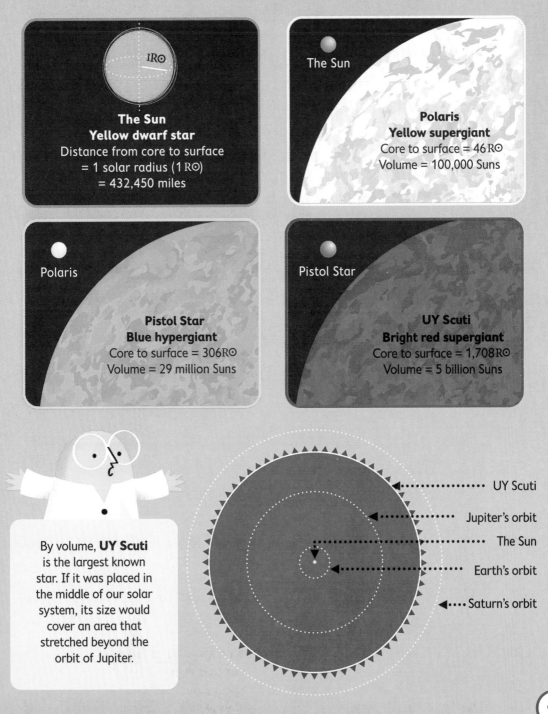

1R☉

The Sun
Yellow dwarf star
Distance from core to surface
= 1 solar radius (1 R☉)
= 432,450 miles

The Sun

Polaris
Yellow supergiant
Core to surface = 46 R☉
Volume = 100,000 Suns

Polaris

Pistol Star
Blue hypergiant
Core to surface = 306 R☉
Volume = 29 million Suns

Pistol Star

UY Scuti
Bright red supergiant
Core to surface = 1,708 R☉
Volume = 5 billion Suns

By volume, **UY Scuti** is the largest known star. If it was placed in the middle of our solar system, its size would cover an area that stretched beyond the orbit of Jupiter.

UY Scuti

Jupiter's orbit

The Sun

Earth's orbit

Saturn's orbit

83 A fireball from space...

hit the Earth but no one noticed.

In 1908, a fragment of asteroid or comet crashed through Earth's atmosphere and exploded in the air, creating a huge fireball. The catastrophic effects were barely noticed, as it exploded above a very remote part of Russia called Tunguska.

33,500 mph
Speed of the object

3,000°F
Temperature of the object

The fireball caused:

4
nights of bright red sky

772 **square miles**
of forest to be destroyed

80
million trees to fall

1,000
reindeer to die

0
human deaths

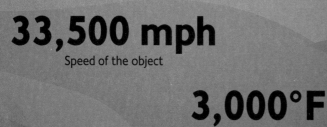

84 Tomato hornworm caterpillars...

inspired an early spacesuit design.

In 1943, engineer **Russell Colley** noticed a caterpillar in his garden.

Colley used this segmented shape in the joints of a new pressure suit.

The caterpillar's body was divided into segments, making it extremely flexible.

This became known as the **Goodrich XH-5** or **tomato worm suit**.

85 It would take 1,500 lifetimes...

to travel to the Sun's nearest star.

The star nearest to the Sun is a red dwarf named Proxima Centauri, about **4.25 light years** away. Flying at the top speed of the Apollo 10 spacecraft, it would take us around **100,000 years** to get there.

Proxima Centauri

100,000 years

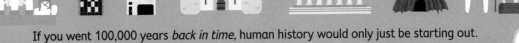

If you went 100,000 years *back in time*, human history would only just be starting out.

Scientists estimate that the Milky Way contains billions of **rogue planets**. These are planets that were ejected from their solar systems – as a result of violent collisions with other planets, for example – and don't orbit any star.

Rogue planets drift endlessly through the dark of interstellar space.

They don't have a star to illuminate them, so they don't have days or nights, seasons or years.

Some rogue planets could actually support life.

On a planet like the one shown here, underwater lifeforms could cluster around plumes of hot minerals and gas, or float through vast caverns.

Icy, rocky crust ········▶

Hot molten core ············▶

Subterranean ocean ··········▶

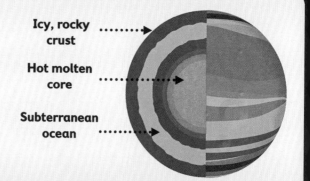

Detecting rogue planets

Astronomers can't see rogue planets, but can detect them using a
phenomenon called **gravity microlensing**. This is when a rogue
planet passes in front of a distant star — and for a moment, its gravity
acts as a lens, **bending** and **magnifying** the star's light.

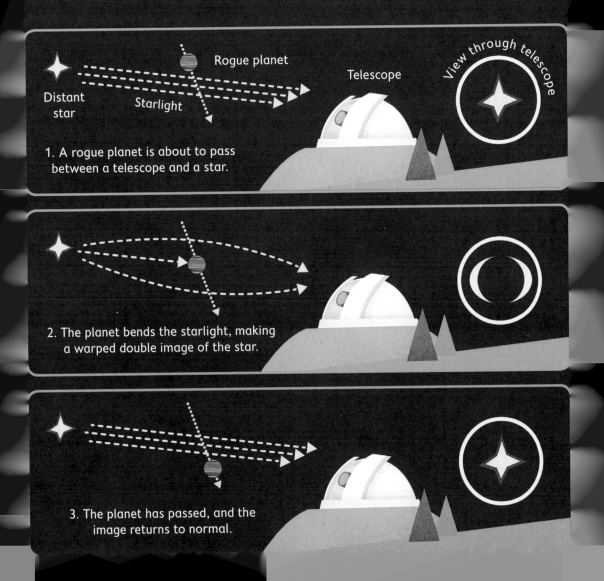

Rogue planet

Telescope

View through telescope

Distant
star

Starlight

1. A rogue planet is about to pass
between a telescope and a star.

2. The planet bends the starlight, making
a warped double image of the star.

3. The planet has passed, and the
image returns to normal.

87 11,000 super tornadoes...

form and collapse on the Sun all the time.

The largest section of the Sun's atmosphere, called the **chromosphere**, is thousands of miles thick. It's made up of fantastically hot, magnetic particles that form gigantic, but short-lived, tornadoes.

Magnetic field: constantly moving

Chromosphere:
upper atmosphere, made up of superhot, magnetized gases known as plasma

Gases at the top of each tornado get pulled up by the magnetic field.

Photosphere:
lower atmosphere, made up of cooling plasma

Gases at the bottom of the tornado sink down into the Sun.

Each tornado only lasts for around

14 minutes

before it dies down.

There are at least

11,000

tornadoes on the Sun at any one moment. A single one could fill an area the **size of the U.S.**

88 The top Soviet rocket designer...

was never, ever mentioned by name.

Sergei Korolev was the Chief Designer of the Soviet Union's rockets and spaceships – but his identity was kept a state secret for fear that foreign agents would try to kidnap or kill him.

1907
Sergei was born in modern-day Ukraine. As a child, he loved gliders and airplanes.

1938
He worked on early rocket technology – but a colleague named Glushko accused him of treason. Sergei went to prison.

1945
He was finally pardoned and put in charge of missile research – working alongside Glushko.

The **Nobel Prize committee** wanted to reward Sputnik's designer, but couldn't because the Soviets refused to reveal his identity.

1957
Sergei designed and launched the very first satellite, called Sputnik.

1953
Sergei began building missiles that could fly up into space and target distant cities.

Sergei was awarded medals that he wasn't allowed to wear in public. He couldn't travel abroad or even appear in photographs.

1961
He designed the Vostok spacecraft that carried the first man into space.

1966
Sergei died during a surgical operation. Only then was his name made public.

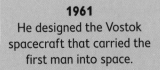

You could drink an asteroid...

or turn it into rocket fuel.

There are millions of asteroids floating through the Solar System. Most are composed of stony rubble, carbon and ice. Some day, this ice could provide drinking water, rocket fuel and air for spacecraft flying from planet to planet.

An electric current splits water **molecules**...

H H
H H O
H H
H H
O O

...into **oxygen**
(used for breathing)

...and **hydrogen**
(used for rocket fuel).

Ice mined from the asteroid is gathered and melted into **water**.

Filters purify the water for drinking.

90 Rockets carry rockets...

in case of emergencies.

Many rockets are designed with a tiny, extra rocket at their very tip, as part of a **Launch Escape System (LES)**. It's only used in emergencies before or during launch, when it can rescue the crew from disaster.

In 1983, a fire broke out on the launch pad of the Soviet Soyuz *T-10-1* spacecraft...

LES tower (containing rocket)

Crew capsule

...so Mission Control activated the LES.

The LES rocket engines ignited, lifting the crew capsule away.

The LES tower and crew capsule flew clear of the launch pad... the tower fell off... and the capsule deployed a parachute for a safe landing.

The two Soviet cosmonauts were saved in the nick of time.

91 The brightest star in the sky...

is actually *two* stars.

To a stargazer on Earth looking up at the night sky, **Sirius**, in the constellation known as *Canis Major*, is brighter than any other star. It looks like a single star, but really it's a **binary star system** – that is, two separate stars, moving around each other.

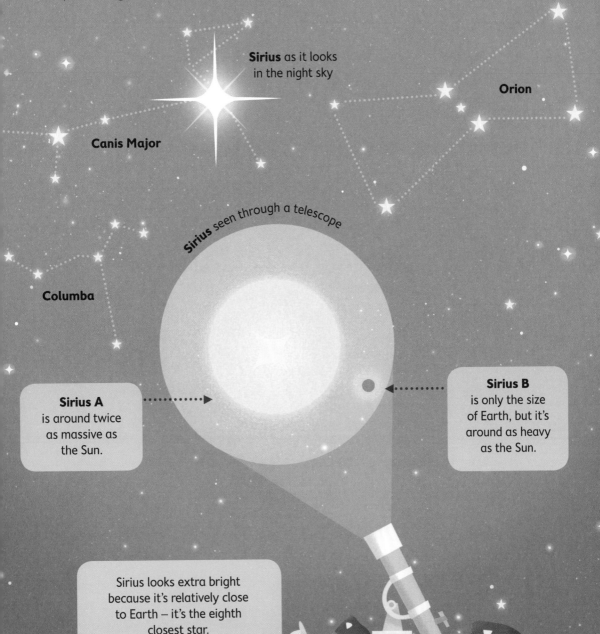

Sirius as it looks in the night sky

Orion

Canis Major

Sirius seen through a telescope

Columba

Sirius A
is around twice as massive as the Sun.

Sirius B
is only the size of Earth, but it's around as heavy as the Sun.

Sirius looks extra bright because it's relatively close to Earth – it's the eighth closest star.

92 Computers in skirts...

plotted routes for early space missions.

During the 1950s, NASA hired a team of female mathematicians to calculate rocket flight paths – by hand. According to **Katherine Johnson**, one of those mathematicians, their role was crucial, but they were seen as little more than *computers who wore skirts*.

To plot space missions, rocket scientists have to take many variables into account. This diagram shows just **eight** of those affecting the Apollo 11 mission.

1 The Earth's rotation

2 The spaceship's acceleration

Spaceship's outward journey

3 The gravitational pull of the Earth

NASA relied on humans to check their calculations, even after they started using electronic computers.

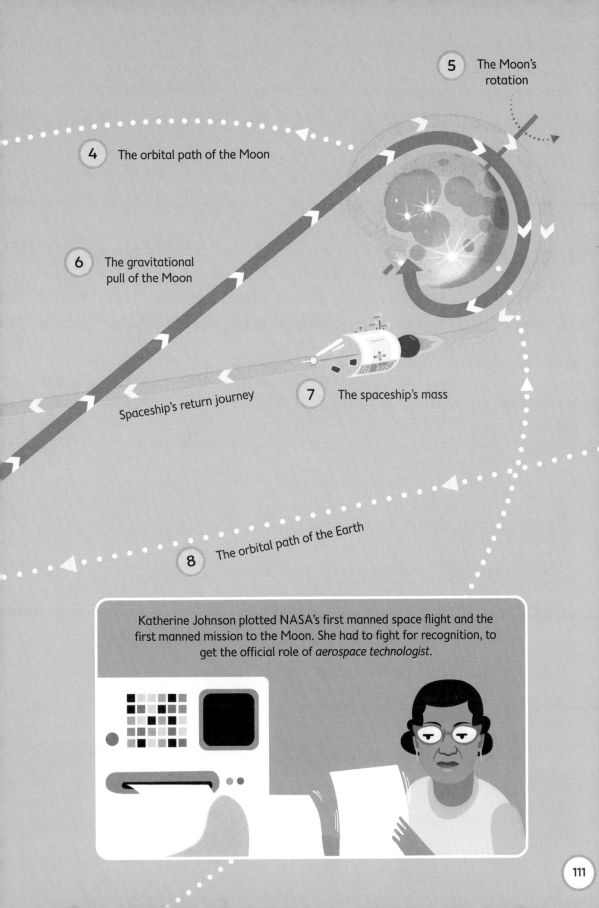

5 The Moon's rotation

4 The orbital path of the Moon

6 The gravitational pull of the Moon

Spaceship's return journey

7 The spaceship's mass

8 The orbital path of the Earth

Katherine Johnson plotted NASA's first manned space flight and the first manned mission to the Moon. She had to fight for recognition, to get the official role of *aerospace technologist*.

Just because we can...
isn't mean we should.

...n it comes to space exploration, there are lots of ethical questions
...nsider. Here are just a few.

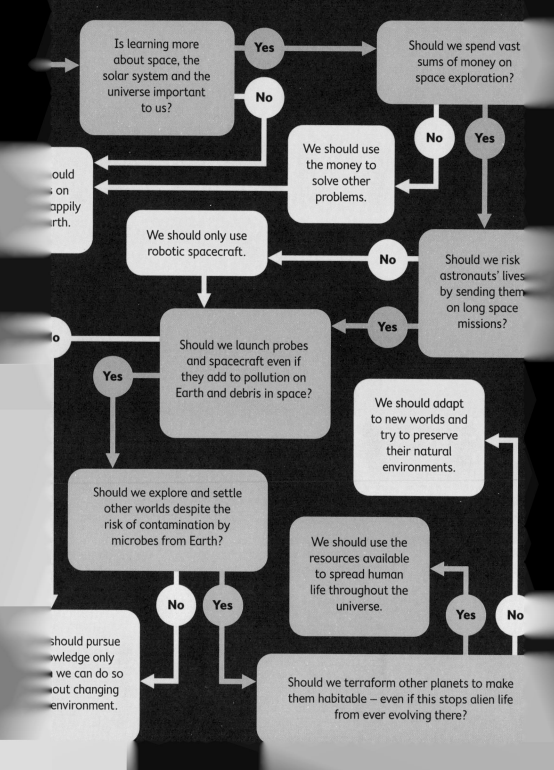

Is learning more about space, the solar system and the universe important to us?

Yes → Should we spend vast sums of money on space exploration?

No

We should use the money to solve other problems.

No / **Yes**

...ould ...s on ...appily ...rth.

We should only use robotic spacecraft.

No ← Should we risk astronauts' lives by sending them on long space missions?

Yes

...o

Yes → Should we launch probes and spacecraft even if they add to pollution on Earth and debris in space?

We should adapt to new worlds and try to preserve their natural environments.

Should we explore and settle other worlds despite the risk of contamination by microbes from Earth?

We should use the resources available to spread human life throughout the universe.

No / **Yes**

Yes / **No**

...should pursue ...owledge only ...n we can do so ...out changing ...environment.

Should we terraform other planets to make them habitable – even if this stops alien life from ever evolving there?

The planet Saturn is famous for the vast, snowy rings of ice and dust that orbit around it. But in fact, rings are quite common. In 2013, astronomers even observed a tiny asteroid with its own set of icy bangles.

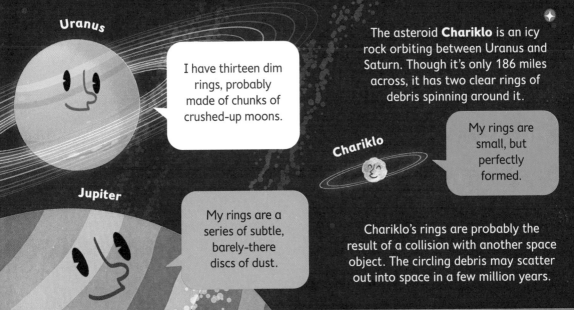

Uranus

I have thirteen dim rings, probably made of chunks of crushed-up moons.

The asteroid **Chariklo** is an icy rock orbiting between Uranus and Saturn. Though it's only 186 miles across, it has two clear rings of debris spinning around it.

Chariklo

My rings are small, but perfectly formed.

Jupiter

My rings are a series of subtle, barely-there discs of dust.

Chariklo's rings are probably the result of a collision with another space object. The circling debris may scatter out into space in a few million years.

95 Outer space can burn you up...

or freeze you solid.

In direct sunlight, an object in space gets so hot it burns up – even if it's millions of miles from the Sun. But as soon as an object falls into shadow, it will start to cool down.

Sun

Losing heat in the vacuum of space takes hours, rather than seconds.

On the sunny side of Venus, a person without a spacesuit would burn up in seconds.

96 Some moots are bigger...

than planets.

Bigger than Mercury	Bigger than Earth's Moon	Bigger than Pluto

Ganymede
Moon of Jupiter
Radius = 1,637 miles

Callisto
Moon of Jupiter
Radius = 1,498 miles

Europa
Moon of Jupiter
Radius = 969 miles

Titan
Moon of Saturn
Radius = 1,600 miles

Io
Moon of Jupiter
Radius = 1,132 miles

Triton
Moon of Neptune
Radius = 841 miles

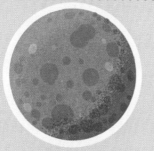

Mercury
Planet
Radius = 1,516 miles

Earth's Moon
Moon of Earth
Radius = 1,080 miles

Pluto
Dwarf planet
Radius = 715 miles

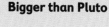

97 Anti-comet umbrellas...

were once sold to protect people from disaster.

Comets are balls of ice, rock and gas that orbit the Sun. In 1910, scientists predicted that the Earth would pass directly through the tail of a comet, called **Halley's Comet**, with deadly consequences.

Scientists had recently discovered that a comet's tail contains poisonous gases such as cyanide.

People thought that the Earth would be suffocated by these deadly gases, and showered with rocky debris.

A market sprang up in protective anti-comet products, from pills to umbrellas.

In the end, nothing bad happened at all.

COMET PILLS

COMET PILLS

THE END is NIGH!

Halley's Comet is named after Sir Edmund Halley. In 1705, he became the first to realize that records of many previous comets were actually describing just one comet which passes Earth every 75 years. Halley's Comet will next be visible in July 2061.

98 The best way to explore Venus...

would be to travel by airship.

The surface of Venus is inhospitable to humans. But up above the clouds, the conditions are similar to the sky on Earth. An airship could keep explorers safe as they sailed through the Venusian skies.

U.S. space agency NASA has long-term plans for a crewed mission to Venus, using inflatable flying machines. It is codenamed **HAVOC** — **H**igh **A**ltitude **V**enus **O**perational **C**oncept.

Average wind speeds on Venus are similar to hurricane-force winds on Earth.

The air on Venus is mostly **carbon dioxide** gas.

Thick dark clouds that hang in the Venusian sky are mostly made of **sulfur dioxide.**

Carbon dioxide in the atmosphere traps heat at cloud level. Temperatures regularly exceed **860°F.**

The atmospheric pressure on the surface is similar to pressure felt at the bottom of Earth's oceans.

Beneath the clouds is a dusty, desert planet, marked by volcanoes.

Rain on Venus is made of deadly **sulfuric acid.**

99 If you discover a comet...

it will be named after you.

More than 6,500 comets have been discovered so far, many by amateur astronomers. So many are found every year that the **International Astronomical Union** has had to create a strict system for naming them.

The first letter shows what **type of comet** it is. This depends on the length of its orbit.

C - a comet with an orbit more than 200 years
P - a comet with an orbit less than 200 years
X - a comet with an unknown orbit

The **year** the comet was found.

C / 2011 W3 (Lovejoy)

The year is split into half-months, coded alphabetically, to narrow down when the comet was discovered.

A is the 1st half of January, and **B** is the 2nd half.
W is the 2nd half of November.
The **3** means it was the 3rd comet to be discovered that half-month.

The last part is the name of the discoverer. Terry Lovejoy, an IT engineer, has discovered five comets from his garden in Australia.

100 In the far future, time will stop...

and the universe will come to an end.

Most astronomers predict that, eventually, all the stars will burn out. The universe itself will be spread so far and wide that there will be no energy for things to move, and no way to measure the passing of time.

It will be utterly cold, all the planets will stop spinning, and there will be no living things anywhere.

This is known as the **heat death of the universe**.

But it won't happen for at least a **googol years** – that's a 1 followed by 100 zeros.

Glossary

This glossary explains some of the words used in this book. Words written in *italic* type have their own entries. For a glossary of space professions, turn to page 123.

Apollo missions A series of missions run by *NASA* with the ultimate goal of sending astronauts to the Moon

asteroid A rock in space that *orbits* a *star*, but is not big enough to be classified as a *planet* or a *dwarf planet*

astronomical unit (AU) A way to measure long distances in space. 1 AU is the distance between the Earth and the Sun.

atmosphere A layer of gases that surrounds a *planet* and some *moons*

atom An incredibly tiny particle; the smallest building block of the solids, liquids and gases that make up all the things in the *universe* that we can see

Big Bang, the A theory about how the *universe* began through the instantaneous appearance and rapid expansion of *matter* from a *singularity*

billion 1,000,000,000

black hole A collapsed *star* that has such a powerful *gravitational pull* that it prevents even light from escaping

capsule The part of a spacecraft that carries astronauts

colonist A person who travels to a new place and tries to settle there permanently

comet A ball of ice and dust in space that *orbits* a *star*

constellation A collection of *stars* that appear to form a pattern

core The central part of a body such as a *planet*

Cosmic Microwave Background The *radiation* remaining from the *Big Bang*, that spreads out to fill the entire *universe*

crater A hole in the surface of a *planet* or *moon* created by the impact of a lump of rock such as a *meteorite*

crust The solid surface layer of a body such as a *planet*

dark matter A substance, not made of *atoms*, that is invisible but is known to have a strong *gravitational pull*

density The amount of *matter* that an object contains, relative to its *volume*

dwarf planet An object in space that *orbits* around the Sun, and may have its own *moons*, but is smaller than a *planet*

eclipse When one object in space is temporarily hidden behind another

ESA European Space Agency, an organization dedicated to the exploration of space

force A push or pull that changes the motion or shape of an object

freefall The experience of falling so fast that it's not possible to fall any faster. Sometimes known as *weightlessness*

galaxy A collection of billions of *stars* that *orbit* together around a central hub

gravitational pull The *force* exerted by one body, such as a *star*, pulling on another, because of its *gravity*

gravity The *force* of two objects pulling on each other; the force that keeps Earth in *orbit* around the Sun

hemisphere Half of a sphere, often refers to the north and south halves of Earth

infrared A kind of light that has slightly less *energy* than red light. It is invisible and not harmful to humans.

intergalactic Of, or to do with, the region of space between two or more galaxies

International Space Station, the (ISS) A vessel that *orbits* around the Earth, where *astronauts* from all countries live and work

interplanetary Of, or to do with, the region of space between *planets* in a *solar system*

interstellar Of, or to do with, the region of space between *stars* in a *galaxy*

lander Part of a *spacecraft* designed to land on a moon or asteroid

laser A beam of intensely powerful light

light year A measure of vast distances in space. **1 light year** is the distance a beam of light travels in a year, roughly 6 *trillion* miles, or 63,000*AU*.

lunar Of, or to do with the Moon

magnetic field The area around a magnet, or a magnetic body such as a *star*, in which objects are affected by that magnet's *force*

mass The total amount of *atoms* that make up a substance

matter The scientific word for stuff

meteorite A rock from space that has landed on the surface of a *planet* or *moon*

microbes Microscopic *organisms* such as bacteria

microwave A type of *radiation* emitted by stars. It cannot be seen, but can be detected by *radio telescopes*.

million 1,000,000

moon A natural body that *orbits* a *planet*

NASA National Aeronautics and Space Administration, the U.S. government agency responsible for space exploration and research

nebula A vast cloud of dust and gases in space that may, over time, pull together to form *stars* and *planets*

neutron star The remains of a massive *star* that has burned out, leaving behind an incredibly *dense* object the size of a *planet*

orbit (verb) To travel through space in a looping path around another, larger object
   (noun) A fixed path taken by an object such as a *satellite* as it travels around a body such as a *planet*

organism Any living thing

PhD A high-level academic qualification. People with PhDs are given the title Doctor.

planet A very large object in space that *orbits* a *star*
   exoplanet A planet that orbits a star in a different *solar system* to Earth's
   rogue planet A planet that wanders through *interstellar space*, and does not orbit any star

plasma Any gas, usually very hot, that has become magnetized because its electrons are released from its *atoms*

pressure The *force* of the *atoms* of one object pushing onto another. For example, the force of gases in Earth's *atmosphere* pushing on a person

probe An unmanned vehicle or machine used to explore a new place, such as space

radiation Particles or rays of energy, including heat and light, given off by a substance such as a *star*
  cosmic radiation Radiation emitted by stars that is deadly for most living things

radio wave A type of *radiation* emitted by *stars* that cannot be seen, but can be detected by *radio telescopes*

red giant A *star* that is cooling down, making it swell up and glow red

rocket A device, full of fuel, that pushes a spacecraft so hard it can escape Earth's *gravitational pull*

rover A robotic vehicle designed to travel along the ground, usually operated by remote control

satellite Any object that *orbits* a *planet*, such as a *moon*, or a machine that sends and receives signals from its host planet

singularity A single point in space and time that once contained all the *matter* in the *universe*

solar system, the The collection of *planets*, *moons* and *asteroids* that *orbit* the Sun

Soviet Union, the A confederation of states, including Russia, that existed between 1922 and 1991, that was one of the main players in the *Space Race*

spacecraft A vehicle that can travel through space

Space Race, the A politically motivated competition between the USA and the *Soviet Union* to see which nation could be the first to send machines and people into space, and then to the Moon, that lasted from 1955 to 1972.

space station A man-made structure in space where people can live and work

star An enormous object in space that continuously fuses its own *atoms* together, creating an incredibly powerful and long-lasting source of heat and light

supercluster An area of the *Universe* made up of *millions* of *galaxies*

supernova The explosion caused by the collapse of a massive *star*, that shines as brightly as a *galaxy* for a few months

telescope A device that can help people see things that are far away
  optical telescope A telescope that detects and enhances visible light using mirrors and lenses
  radio telescope A telescope that detects invisible forms of *radiation*, such as *microwaves* or *radio waves*

thrust A force that pushes an object, such as a *rocket* launching from Earth

trillion 1,000,000,000,000

universe, the Everything that exists in time and space
  the known universe A part of the whole *universe*, that people can detect using instruments based on or around planet Earth. Also called **the observable universe**

volcano A hole in a *planet's* or *moon's* crust caused by an eruption of hot liquid from beneath the surface

volume The amount of space taken up by an object

wavelength Energy, such as light from *stars*, travels in waves of different lengths. The wavelength determines the form the *radiation* takes, such as visible light.

weightlessness The sensation of being in *freefall*, which feels like floating

white dwarf A *star* near the end of its life that is no longer producing new heat, but is still glowing

Glossary of space professionals

Space is not only a huge place – it's also a very wide field of study. This list includes just a few of the different jobs that people do to learn about space.

archaeoastronomer Someone who studies the history of *astronomy*

astrobiologist Someone who studies *organisms* in space, or on *planets* and *moons*

astrochemist Someone who studies substances found in *stars*, *planets*, *moons*, *asteroids* and *comets*

astronaut A person whose job involves going into *space*. Also known as a **cosmonaut** in Russia, or a **taikonaut** in China

astronomer Someone who studies space, usually using optical *telescopes* or radio telescopes to detect distant objects

astrophysicist Someone who studies how *stars* work

cosmologist Someone who studies how the *universe* began, and how it will end

engineer Someone who designs and creates buildings or vehicles
  aeronautical engineer An engineer who works on vehicles designed to leave Earth's *atmosphere*, such as *rockets* and *spacecraft*

flight controller One of a large team that plans and monitors space missions from launch to landing

flight surgeon A doctor who looks after *astronauts* in training, and monitors their health while they are on space missions

planetary scientist Someone who studies *planets*, *moons* and *solar systems*
  atmospheric scientist Someone who studies *atmospheres*, especially on alien planets and moons
  exoplanetologist Someone who studies planets beyond Earth's solar system

Index

A

absolute zero, 15, 63
Adams, John Couch, 68
aerodynamic shapes, 64
airships, 116
Aldrin, Buzz, 26, 45
aliens, 30, 33, 79
Anaxagoras, 33
Ancient Greeks, 39
Andromeda, 20, 70
ants, 26
Apollo missions, 50-51, 88
    Apollo 8, 45
    Apollo 11, 26, 28, 32, 45, 66
    Apollo 14, 92
    Apollo 17, 29
Arecibo message, 79
Armstrong, Neil, 28, 45, 66
Arrhenius, Svante, 33
Asteroid Belt, 12, 31
asteroids, 12-13, 14, 31, 33, 48, 49, 55, 80, 100, 106-107, 113
astronauts, 8, 9, 22, 23, 28-29, 37, 38-39, 44, 45, 50, 51, 53, 62, 71, 91, 92
astronomers, 30, 47, 74, 75, 76, 79, 118
astronomical units (AU), 20-21
astrophysicists, 59, 89
atmospheres, 55, 73, 82-83, 84, 85, 117

B

bears, 86
Big Bang, the, 18, 75
binary stars, 109
black holes, 5, 77
Bouvard, Alexis, 68

C

Callisto, 114
Canis major, 109
capsules, 82, 86
carbon dioxide, 55, 85, 116
caterpillars, 101
Cernan, Eugene, 29
chimpanzees, 22
clouds, 25, 117
cold, 15, 113
Colley, Russell, 101
colonization, 54, 55, 94-95, 112
comets, 14, 80, 100, 115, 118
computers, 110-111
constellations, 65, 109
cores, 43, 57, 76, 90
Cosmic Microwave Background, 75
cosmonauts, 44, 45, 86-87, 108
costs, 62, 112
craters, 24, 15, 78
Curiosity rover, 27

D

dangers of space, 72-73
dark matter, 58-59, 60
days, 96
diamonds, 14, 43
dinosaurs, 24
dogs, 22
Drake Equation, 30
Drake, Frank, 30
dwarf planets, 12-13

E

Earth, 4, 33, 40, 48, 96
eclipses, 19
EMU, 23
ethics, 112

Europa, 94-95, 114
event horizon, 77
exosphere, 84
extremophiles, 33

F

fireball, 100
food, 38-39, 54, 61, 88
footprints, 51
former planets, 12-13
fourth dimension, the, 34
freefall, 36-37
fruit flies, 22
fusion of metals, 91

G

Gagarin, Yuri, 22, 44
galaxies, 6-7, 58-59, 70
Galileo, 98
Galle, Johann, 68
Ganymede, 114
Gemini III, 61
geocentrism, 98
global warming, 55
gold, 14, 23, 43
golf, 67, 92
graveyard orbit, 97
gravity, 36, 58, 77, 96, 92-93, 103, 110
Gray, Kathryn Aurora, 56
Grissom, Gus, 61

H

Halley, Edmund, 115
Halley's comet, 115
heat, 42, 43, 57, 90, 104, 103
heat death, 119
heliocentrism, 98
helioseismology, 76
hibernation, 53, 63
Hoffleit, Dorrit, 11

hydrogen, 57, 74, 106
hypercubes, 34

I

ice, 14, 27, 54, 85
intergalactic space, 14
International Astronomical
    Union, 118
International Space Station,
    see ISS
inventions, 88
invisibility, 17, 58-59, 64
Io, 114
Iron, 43
ISS, 8-9, 23, 36, 38, 52,
    62, 71

J

jetpacks, 23
Johnson, Katherine, 111
junk, 97
Jupiter, 57, 94, 98, 113

K

Kármán Line, 84
Kelvin, Lord, 33
known universe, 7, 21
Korolev, Sergei, 105

L

landing, 26, 28-29, 82-83
lasers, 64
Launch Escape System, 108
Leonov, Alexei, 45
Le Verrier, Urbain, 68
life on other planets, 27, 30,
    33, 54, 55, 94-95, 102, 116
life, origins of, 33
life, search for, 27, 30, 79

light, 16, 17, 59, 82-83, 90,
    103
light years, 20-21, 65, 101
living in space, 9, 18-19, 23,
    28-29, 38-39, 53, 61, 62, 71
Lovejoy, Terry, 118
Luna 9, 45
lunar modules, 28, 51

M

magnetic fields, 73, 104
man in the Moon, 78
Mars, 14, 27, 52, 53, 54, 55,
    85, 82-83
Mars Climate Orbiter, 69
Maya, the, 10
Mercury, 96, 114
metals, 91
meteorites, 50
meteoroids, 24
metric system, 69
microwaves, 16, 75
Milky Way, the, 5, 6, 20, 70
minor planets, 12
Miranda, 96
monkeys, 22
Moon, the, 14, 15, 19, 24, 26,
    28-29, 44-45, 50-51, 78,
    92-93, 111, 114
Moon dust, 50-51
moons, 80-81, 98, 114
moss piglets, 63

N

NASA, 35, 61, 62, 69, 97,
    110, 111
Neptune, 20, 68
neutron stars, 47, 60
night sky, 11, 17

O

Oberth, Herman, 32
observatories, 56
Oort Cloud, the, 20, 21
Opportunity rover, 82-83
orbits, 4, 5, 9, 36, 37, 52, 69,
    80-81, 96, 97, 98, 111, 113
Orion, 65
oxygen, 27, 55, 64, 72, 106

P

panspermia, 33
Payne-Gaposchkin, Cecilia, 74
pepper, 38
physics, laws of, 18
pigeons, 75
Pistol Star, 99
planets, 5, 12-13, 30, 98, 102
plasma, 40, 76
Pluto, 13, 20, 114
Polaris, 99
pressure, 49, 63, 72, 117
Proxima Centauri, 20, 101

Q

quarantine, 26

R

rabbits, 22
radiation, 49, 63, 73
radio telescopes, 16, 75, 79
radio waves, 16
raspberries, 25
red supergiants, 47, 99
rings, 80-81, 113
robots, 27, 62, 66, 82-83, 88
rocket fuel, 42, 106
rockets, 32, 35, 42, 43, 44,
    52, 105, 108

rocket science, 110
rogue planets, 102-103
rotation, planetary, 4, 96,
   110
Royal Astronomical Society,
   the, 60
Russell, Henry, 74
Russia, 86-87, 100
Russian language, 8

S

Sagittarius B2, 25
sandwich, corned beef, 61
satellites, 36, 44, 46, 84, 97
Saturn, 14, 80-81, 113
Saturn V rocket, 32
Shepard, Alan, 44, 92
singularity, 18
Sirius, 109
snow, 85, 86-87
solar radius, 99
solar system, the, 5, 12-13,
   20-21, 31, 57
sound, 64, 76
Soviet Union, the, 32, 44-45,
   105
Soyuz, 108
space boots, 51, 66
spacecraft, 22, 31, 32, 35,
   36, 37, 44-45, 52, 53,
   62, 64, 67, 69, 77, 84, 97,
   101, 105, 108, 110-111
Space Race, the, 32, 44-45
space stations, 18-19, 36,
   38-39, 75
spacesuits, 23, 50, 62, 73,
   101, 113
space travel, 22, 26, 28-29,
   32, 36, 44-45, 52-53, 61,
   62, 84, 101, 108, 110, 112
spacewalking, 23, 45, 86
spaghettification, 77
speed of light, 64, 77

speed of sound, 42
spies, 46
Sputnik, 44, 105
stars, 6, 11, 16, 17, 47, 58,
   65, 77, 98, 99
Sun, the, 4, 40-41, 43, 74, 76,
   82-83, 90, 99, 104
sunsets, 9
superclusters, 6-7
supergalaxies, 70
supernova, 56, 60
Syracuse, 39

T

tardigrades, 63
Tareshkova, Valentina, 44
telescopes, 16, 56, 68, 75, 79,
   98, 103, 109
temperatures, 42, 43, 63
terraforming, 55
Thorne, Kip, 47
Thorne-Żytkow objects, 47
thrust, 36
time, 34, 119
time travel, 89
Titan, 114
toilets, 62
tornadoes, 104
Triton, 114
Tunguska, 100

U

Ukraine, 105
umbrellas, 115
United States, 32, 44-45
universe, the, 4-7, 17, 20,
   38, 119
Uranus, 68, 96, 113
UY Scuti, 99

V

V-2 rocket, 32
Velcro®, 23, 39
Venus, 10, 113, 116-117
volcanoes, 24, 43, 117
von Braun, Wernher, 32
Vostok, 105
Voyager 1, 20

W

water, 27, 71, 85, 94, 106
wavelengths, 16, 17
weapons, 87
weather, 35, 85, 104, 117
weightlessness, 37, 38-39
Wickramasinghe, Chandra, 33
wolves, 86-87
wormholes, 89

Y

years, 4, 5, 96
Young, John, 61

Z

Zwicky, Fritz, 60
Żytkow, Anna, 47

Internet links

For links to websites where you can discover more surprising space facts, watch astronauts at work and see inside spacecraft, go to the Usborne Quicklinks website at **usborne.com/Quicklinks** and enter the keywords: **100 space things**.

Here are some of the things you can do at the websites we recommend:

- zoom into images of stars and galaxies
- find out about a lander that's been put on a comet
- examine a replica of the Mars rover, *Curiosity*
- listen to sounds from space
- find out how to spot the ISS in the night sky

The recommended websites are regularly reviewed and updated but, please note, Usborne Publishing is not responsible for the content of any website other than its own. We recommend that children are supervised while on the internet.

Getting any mission off the ground...

requires a team of dedicated people.

Research & Writing
Alex Frith
Alice James
Jerome Martin

Layout & Design
Matthew Bromley
Lenka Hrehova
Stephen Moncrieff
Hayley Wells

Illustration
Federico Mariani
Shaw Nielsen

Series editor
Ruth Brocklehurst

Space expert
Nick Howes

Additional editorial material Matthew
Oldham and Hazel Maskell